RYAN HUNT

Self-Discipline

The Spartan and Special Operations Way To Mastering Yourself

Copyright © 2018 by Ryan Hunt

First edition

This book was professionally typeset on Reedsy.
Find out more at reedsy.com

Contents

Introduction   iv

The Spartans and Special Operations Units   1

The Science and Psychology of Self-Discipline   15

Developing Self-Discipline   26

Self-Discipline and Freedom   38

Building Mental Toughness   44

Improving Focus and Concentration   56

Forming Good Habits and Breaking Bad Habits   67

Fearlessness and Overcoming Fear   80

Lessons Learned from the Spartans and Special Forces   90

Daily Self-Discipline—Applying What You Have Learned in Your...   99

Conclusion   109

Thank You   111

Copyright   112

Introduction

You want to wake up early in the morning to be more productive but you always end up pressing that snooze button on your alarm. You want to stop buying things that you don't really need but you always find yourself maxing out your credit card. You want to lose weight and just become a healthier individual but you just cannot stop yourself from ordering at a nearby fast food. You really think you need to go to the gym and get in shape but you just find it so hard to spend an extra hour to exercise especially after work. Everything just feels so difficult to do.

You know what you need? Self-discipline. And the good thing is you are not alone in this constant battle against temptations and impulses. Misery does love company. A lot of people suffer from the same predicament. They always have the best goals and objectives to make them successful in life but they always end up not doing it.

Lucky for you, this book will be your companion and ally in your daily struggles of resisting temptations. It will tell you all about how inspiring and amazing groups of people, such as the Spartans and Special Operations Units, practiced self-discipline in order for them to achieve their goals and complete their missions. If you feel like giving up, always remember that these strong people had to face more difficult challenges but their discipline never wavered.

This book will not only teach you how the Spartans and Special Operations Units trained but will also show you how they become the epitome of self-disciplined individuals.

We also look at the science and psychology of self-discipline and how you can improve it to become successful in life.

1

The Spartans and Special Operations Units

If you are searching for someone to look up to when it comes to improving your self-discipline, you can choose between the Spartans and the different special operations units, or you can choose both since both groups of men have exemplary self-discipline and willpower.

The Spartans

Sparta was an ancient Greek society that placed a high value on its military prowess, with boys starting military training at the young age of 7. When Sparta defeated Athens, its rival city-state in the Peloponnesian War, it became one of the most powerful cities during its time. This can be attributed to the fact that the Spartan culture was mainly focused on military service and loyalty to the state. At the age of 7, young boys started their military training sponsored by the state. They followed the Agoge system which puts emphasis on endurance, duty, courage, obedience, and of course, discipline.

Although there was no need for Spartan women to undergo military training like men, they were still highly athletic and physically strong. They were also more educated and enjoyed independence and higher status than the rest of the women in Greece.

Since men in Sparta spent all their lives training for the military to serve the state, and later became professional soldiers, all manual labor that was necessary for the survival of any society was assigned to the Helots, a slave class in the city. Another group of people who lived in the city was the Perioeci, which literally means "dwellers-around". These were the people who were neither professional soldiers nor slaves and worked as traders and craftsmen.

They were also the ones responsible for building the weapons used by the Spartan soldiers. This division in the society only shows that the state did not want its soldiers to be distracted by other things. They only wanted them to focus solely on their military training, which is no wonder why the Spartans, up to now, are known for their military strength.

The Agoge system

As mentioned previously, the Spartans followed a rigorous education system called the Agoge system which was mainly centered on self-control, courage, obedience, and endurance, to name a few. The word 'Agoge' literally means 'rearing' in English. Agoge was a controversial education system even during the ancient times because of how rigorous and intensive it was. However, it was a requirement for all Spartans to receive Spartan citizenship. The main goal of the Agoge system was to have brave and strong soldiers who could protect the state in times of adversity.

Unlike other Greek states, public education was provided by the Spartan government. Young children, both males and females, had to complete said education, although they were taught and trained in different manners. Only the royal heirs were exempted from this requirement.

To understand more about the Agoge system, here is a brief outline.

- **Birth to 7 years of age**

The Agoge values were instilled in the minds of the Spartans as early as infancy. After birth, the mother would bathe the infant in wine because they believed that wine would make a child strong. The infant had to undergo inspection by the elders of the city, called the *Gerousia*, to determine whether the child was healthy and strong. They only wanted healthy and strong babies.

If the infant passed the inspection with flying colors, he would be sent back home with his parents. If the elders found any kind of birth defect or deformity or signs that the baby would grow up weak, the parents had to abandon the baby at once. These babies were left to die alone or were sometimes rescued by strangers. Some even said that weak babies were thrown off a cliff, while others claimed that the babies were left alone on the cliff and if they survived, it meant they were worthy to become a Spartan.

Growing up, children were not cuddled and showered with TLC, which is what modern parents do to their children. Spartan children experienced tough love from their parents. Instead of bathing them with warm water, the children were bathed in wine. Instead of picking them up when they started to cry, the babies were often ignored.

Instead of reading them children's stories and singing them lullabies, the Spartan parents started to plant the seeds of the Agoge system in the minds of their young ones, telling them that they were not worthy of becoming a Spartan if they did not become the strongest and bravest men who could protect their city. Children were also taught that fear was a sign of weakness. This extreme parenting approach was known far and wide in ancient Greece, which is why elite families outside Sparta would often hire Spartan women to become caretakers of their children.

· *Age 7 to 20*

Officially, the Agoge system started when a young boy turned 7, unlike today when kids are expected to leave their homes at the age of 18. When they started the Agoge system, they became under complete control of the government because the training and education were financed by the state. The boys were sent in groups and they had to live with a group of older men who would serve as their mentors.

The children were housed in a dormitory and were educated in a communal barracks. The subjects ranged from academics and sports to hunting and warfare. Their education was military-oriented because they were basically grooming the children to become soldiers.

When the boys reached the age of 12, they were given only one piece of clothing, specifically a red cloak that they had to use no matter what the weather conditions were. The reason behind this was that they would be able to withstand even the harshest of weather conditions without being dependent on clothing, which would turn them into tough soldiers. They would also be barefoot when they did any kind of sports or physical activities such as gymnastics.

Their food was also strictly rationed, much stricter than in a modern-day prison because the Agoge system used hunger and thirst to promote self-discipline. You might think this is a little too much and can be considered inhumane by today's standards. However, keep in mind that the intention was not to torture these children or to give them a difficult life but to prepare them for when they would become full-fledged soldiers and scarcity of water and food while in a battle was a common occurrence. Feeding them less also made their bodies leaner and more fit to endure hard physical activities.

Young Spartan boys were also taught to make their own beds—literally. They had to get the materials such as straws and reeds from the banks of the Eurotas river without using a knife. Another interesting thing about the Agoge system was that the boys were encouraged to steal as long as they didn't get caught. If they were caught, they were given severe punishments. This helped develop stealth that proved useful when it became necessary to steal supplies and provisions from the enemy.

To bring out the toughness of these young boys, the elders in the barracks instigated fights among the young students. Whoever lost would be made fun of and ridiculed because they were seen as weak and cowardly. In fact, some records show that every year, adolescent students had to undergo an endurance test where many died. To honor those students who successfully passed the test, they were given wreaths, a symbol of victory in Greece in the olden times.

Do not think that the Agoge system was all about physical strength and discipline. Other areas that were taught to the students include reading, writing, history, singing, dancing, war poems, and literature. They were even required to study the works of Homer. This made it a little similar to a typical modern-day education system.

When the boys reached the age of 18, they began serving in the Spartan Army as military reserves. There were some who became members, specifically spies, of the Secret Police force of Sparta. They had to spy on the Helots, or the slave class, and report them to the authority if they are doing something against the government. They were also licensed to kill.

· *Age 20 to 30*

The Agoge training officially ended when the male students turned 20 years of age. At this point when they were already considered as adults, they became official members of the Spartan Army and they had to undergo professional military training under the army.

The men had to become a member of a *Syssitia*, a military-style mess where they had to undergo training for war. The members of the mess, who were also Spartans, had to elect members from the newcomers. Aside from military training, the *Syssitia was* also involved in the granting of citizenship. It was extremely important for the student to be elected and become a part of a mess if he wanted to secure Spartan citizenship. The election all depended on the unanimous votes of the old members.

When a man became a citizen of Sparta, he would be able to do things that non-citizens did not have the right to do such as voting, marrying, and running for public office. Some soldiers married before the completion of the training, meaning before the age of 30, but they were banned from living in the same house as their wife. It was possible to not get elected into a mess. Men who were still not members of a mess even after 10 years of completing the Agoge, would not be able to secure citizenship.

The military training in the *Syssitia* ended when a man reached the age of 30. But a Spartan man had to be a soldier until retirement at the age of 60, or until the day he died.

Education for females

Unlike other cities in Greece, Spartan women were highly educated. Although the State also sponsored their education, it was not as demanding and as rigorous as the education for boys, although the focus was also on the military. If boys were groomed to become soldiers, girls were trained to become mothers of a true Spartan soldier.

They did not need to go to a dormitory away from their families. They lived with their parents while attending school. They had subjects that would make them physically strong such as gymnastics, sports, and dancing. If they were strong physically, they would also be strong enough to give birth to strong babies. They were also taught subjects about war and combat.

Females were also trained to help male students in their military training. What kind of help, you ask. The girls motivated the boys to do their best by teasing, humiliating and ridiculing them in public if they were not performing well during physical activity such as sports or exercising. The girls would create a list of the men who they thought were under-performing so that they could shame and humiliate them to motivate them to be and do better. They were also taught typical school subjects such as poetry, history, and music.

At the age of 20, the education of girls would be officially completed, and they were then expected to find a partner to marry. They were encouraged to find mates who were physically strong and courageous who could in turn help them bring out a future Spartan warrior into the world. Marriage was not seen as a union of two individuals who were in love, but rather as a way to produce warriors who were brave and strong and who could protect the State from enemies and invasion.

As what could be observed, the Spartans had a do-or-die approach when it came to their education and training, and also in everything else they did. Mediocrity was not tolerated. It's either they were the best soldiers or they had to leave. You are probably thinking right now that the Agoge system is too much and is kind of extreme, especially in these modern times.

However, you have to understand that the period when they lived was very different from today. It was a turbulent time where battles and invasions were a common occurrence in their daily lives. And if they were ill-prepared, they would not have a chance at all. Although the entire approach is no longer suitable to today's standards, you can still learn a lot from how the Spartans trained their soldiers, especially when it comes to developing self-discipline and willpower.

The Special Operations Units

Today, what comes close to the Spartan way of training is the training of the Special Operations Units or Special Forces. Some examples of these elite groups are the Special Air Service (SAS), Navy Seals, Green Berets, Special Boat Service (SBS), and US Marine Raiders. They are involved in high profile operations which is why their training is also more demanding than the regular military troops.

In any military setting, discipline and obedience are an integral part of their day to day work routine if they want to successfully accomplish their missions. Following each and every step is crucial because it affects not only all military operations but also the civilians. Soldiers are taught to be obedient to authority and regulations at all times and also to always observe strict self-discipline that will result in excellent performance, which means minimizing dangers to both the soldiers and the civilians.

Military Discipline and Self-discipline

Soldiers are taught to be disciplined and obedient. They have to follow authority, commands, and rules without question. If they question the authority, then it becomes a problem. To be considered well-disciplined, the team has to follow orders whether they like it or not, and no matter how unpleasant and dangerous the task at hand is.

Total compliance is required to achieve efficiency within the organization. Disorganization and disobedience in the team are dangerous and can put the lives of the other group members at risk. The survival of special forces units depends a lot on the obedience of the team to a centralized command and the self-discipline of each and every member.

Military self-discipline is achieved when the soldier starts to see himself as an integral instrument to achieve the organization's mission. This internal-ization involves acceptance of regulation and obedience to a higher authority. Soldiers who are self-disciplined know how to control themselves and always make decisions based on how it will affect the entire organization. They also do not need constant external supervision because they know how to keep themselves in line.

When a soldier has self-discipline, obedience comes from within and not from coercion or another form of external force. Those soldiers who exhibit strong willpower and self-discipline are viewed by their superior as reliable. The higher-ups know that these soldiers can perform their duty correctly and willingly, without the need to use force or coercion. These highly disciplined soldiers are the ones who move up to become members of the highly elite special forces or special operations units.

Special Forces Training

Of course, the different units of the elite Special Forces have different kinds of training but they are more or less the same. They are all physically, mentally, and emotionally demanding, exhausting, and intensive. Their training is a lot more difficult than the training of regular soldiers. This is because they will be assigned to work in high-risk and high-profile operations that affect not only their own country but the whole world.

The Special Forces training is the toughest training and testing platform in the Military. It is a year-long process (or longer) that is designed to break even the toughest soldiers. In fact, it is so difficult to pass that only 10% of the candidates successfully finish the entire process.

Once you enter the training, you only have three options—to quit, get injured, or outlast—and of course the third option is the only option if you want to become a member of the Special Operations group. You are probably wondering how can an individual survive such training if it is designed to break even the toughest person?

Keep in mind that the human body is a wonderful machine and can adapt in almost all kinds of situations—heat, cold, pain, and stress. Someone who is tough means that his body and also his mind and emotions are highly adaptable and do not easily give up because he knows that it is possible to successfully complete the training. More often than not, it is mind over matter.

The training also puts a lot of emphasis on mental strength aside from physical strength. If the body is strong enough to withstand pain and discomfort, it becomes easy to develop mental strength.

· *The right mindset*

Members of these Special Forces Units are highly self-disciplined because they have the right mindset. Self-discipline has more to do with mental toughness than physical toughness, although mental toughness becomes easier to achieve if the body is also strong.

If you want to be successful in life, you have to stick it out until the end even when things become too hard to handle. This is something that the Special Forces have—when the going gets tough, they still continue doing their mission, something that the rest of the society should learn.

The world you live in today is filled with softies who get offended at the smallest things and if you develop mental toughness like the Special Forces, then you have an advantage over all these people. You are setting yourself up for success when you have the mindset to stick it out while the rest is giving up.

· *Physical training*

The Special Forces Units have to undergo intensive physical training, as you already know by now. The kind of physical training that they do require a lot more than being strong and healthy. To be able to successfully do all the physical tests, you have to have commitment and self-discipline. Principles included in the training are work capacity, calisthenics or gymnastics, resistance training, and endurance, to name a few.

This kind of training gives Special Forces soldiers a strong and athletic body that is well-rounded and can perform well in any kind of weather and environment and even in extremely stressful situations.

You do not necessarily need to follow the difficult training of the Spartans and the Special Forces Units and you do not need to train at that level because you are just an ordinary person who wants to improve your life by obtaining self-discipline. However, the information and facts shared in this chapter will at least give you an idea how the Spartans and Special Forces train. This training greatly improves their self-discipline, and you can use what you have learned to greatly improve your self-discipline. At least you know one thing now—being successful takes a lot of hard work and effort on your part. It is not a walk in the park.

2

The Science and Psychology of Self-Discipline

One of the most famous psychological tests is the marshmallow test, which you are probably very familiar with. It is a part of a series of studies on willpower and delayed gratification. The studies were conducted by a Stanford professor Walter Mischel in the 60s and 70s. Even back then, experts were very much interested in understanding willpower. And up to now, psychologists and scientists still conduct studies about it because it holds the key to a successful life.

Willpower gives us self-discipline. It is what prevents us from spending all our money buying things that we like and instead of putting them in a savings account for the future. It is what makes us go to work and finish our job before the deadline or study for an exam even when all we want to do is watch TV or sleep. It is what pushes us to eat healthy and spend an hour at the gym exercising. It is what makes us say no to temptations, temptations that will give us instant gratification but will sabotage our future.

No wonder scientists and psychologists continue to study willpower and self-discipline. It is what makes a person successful. They want to understand what makes a person more disciplined than the next person, and in what situation and what is the reasoning behind it. What exactly is going on in the brain, chemically speaking, when a person summons up his willpower to force himself to do things he really does not want to do to get his reward later on, and also when a person just gives up and says, to hell with it? These have been topics of discussion and research for decades.

Components of achieving goals

Although willpower and self-discipline are considered the key to a successful life, other things also play important roles in achieving goals and objectives. The first thing that you need to do is to know your motivation and set a clear goal. The Spartans, for instance, were motivated to undergo the training because they wanted to become citizens and also to be someone worthy in the eyes of their people.

The Special Forces are motivated because they know that they are going to be a part of an elite team that plays an important role in world issues and conflicts. Your motivation can be something as simple as wanting to provide a good life for your family or wanting to look and feel good.

The second component is monitoring your behavior towards that goal. You have to want it badly enough to be able to endure hardships and challenges that you might encounter in trying to achieve your goal. Your behavior should not change while in the process of achieving your goal. Otherwise, you will lose the reason why you are doing all of those things in the first place.

And finally, the third component of achieving goals is willpower that leads to self-discipline. You cannot achieve your goal without the willpower to overcome temptations. Whether it is saying no to another chocolate bar, not watching random YouTube videos, or stopping yourself from buying something just because it is on sale, willpower plays an important role in all this.

The energy model of self-control

This is one of the popular theories about willpower and self-discipline, which states that the brain works like a muscle. It has a supply of strength or energy that is limited and can be used up through exertion. This is why we have lapses when it comes to willpower. We are not self-disciplined at all times because our mental energy for self-control gets depleted, also called ego depletion.

If you have used up your mental energy by practicing willpower and self-control to do one particular task, then it might be difficult to be as disciplined as before with subsequent challenges. This is the reason why we are more prone to give in to instant gratification, such as going on a shopping spree or eating sweets, when we are feeling stressed. It suffers from fatigue after usage but just like an ordinary muscle, it can also be strengthened through exercise, meaning you have to continue using it again and again to make your willpower stronger. The effect of fatigue is instant while the effect of strengthening the muscle is delayed.

There was an experiment conducted to show that willpower is a limited resource. Two groups of individuals were placed in the same room, one group was given a bowl of cookies that were freshly baked and smelled really good, and the other group was given a bowl of radishes. The first group was told to eat the cookies and the second group was told to eat the radishes.

After some time, the participants were given a puzzle to solve. And not surprisingly, those who ate cookies kept working on the puzzle for 20 minutes while those who ate the radishes only lasted a measly 8 minutes. The explanation behind this is that the participants who ate the radishes already used their brain energy or willpower to resist eating the delicious-smelling cookies. They did not have any more energy reserves to continue solving the puzzle.

But aside from exerting willpower again and again, the brain also suffers more from the so-called ego depletion when they are practicing self-discipline to please others and not to achieve personal goals and desires. This is why it is best to set clear goals that will benefit yourself and not to impress others.

According to the proponents of this theory, mental energy can be refueled by simply providing your brain with sugar or other simple carbohydrates. This model has been tremendously influential in a lot of succeeding studies about willpower and self-discipline.

But what actually gets depleted when a person no longer has the energy to control himself? Willpower is a term used to describe psychological processes that are happening in the brain, but what exactly is the scientific process? Glucose plays an important role in this theory. It acts as a fuel that helps the brain perform mental activities efficiently. Anything that your body does is fueled by glucose—muscular exertion and the function of the immune system. Neurotransmitters are also composed of glucose. Glucose comes from sugar and also other nutritious foods. It is either used right away or stored as energy reserves for later use.

However, it cannot be said that it is the be-all and end-all explanation. There is more to self-discipline than refueling the brain with sugar.

Defining Self-Discipline

Self-discipline can be used interchangeably with these terms: willpower, drive, determination, self-control, and resolve. But what exactly is self-discipline? It is a person's ability to not give in to impulses, behaviors, and emotions that will give instant rewards in order to achieve long-term goals.

This is what separates humans from animals, which has a scientific basis because the whole process of willpower and self-discipline happens in the pre-frontal cortex of the brain, which is a lot bigger in humans than in animals, particularly other mammals with the same kind of brain structure. Some scientists even go as far as claiming that self-discipline is what makes humans human. This allows humans to plan and analyze alternative courses of action instead of doing whatever they feel like doing that can only lead to regret. It is the ability to wait for a bigger reward by forgoing small and easy rewards.

It is also the capacity to remove any unwanted feeling, thought, or impulse, especially when you are having a difficult time. The Spartans and Special Forces probably have thought about quitting or giving up during the difficult training but they have the mental strength not to give up because they focus their sight on their goals.

There are three different aspects of willpower, or self-discipline: the ability to resist impulses and temptations or the "I won't" power , the ability to do things that have to be done or the "I will" power, and the awareness of your personal desires and goals or the "I want" power. You have to use all these three not only to achieve your goals but also to steer clear of trouble.

Self-discipline is a form of effortful and conscious regulation of one's self by one's self. It is all about fighting temptations, resisting impulses, and using different kinds of techniques to be in control. No wonder it is a tiring activity because your enemy is your own self.

Delaying gratification

The popular marshmallow experiment stated previously is a prime example of delayed gratification. Willpower is basically that, the ability of an individual to delay gratification. The lead researcher gave a more detailed explanation using the hot and cool systems.

The cool system is a thinking system responsible for analyzing feelings, actions, and sensations. It is a reflective system that reminds you why you should not eat that marshmallow right away.

Then there is the hot system, which is emotional and impulsive and reacts quickly to external stimuli and triggers, such as eating the marshmallow right away because you know how fluffy and sweet it would taste and feel in your mouth. Just think of it this way, the cool system is the angel and the hot system is the devil.

When the hot system overrides the cool system in your brain, meaning your willpower fails, you give in to temptations and impulses because it makes you feel good at that instant. According to these studies, some people are more sensitive to impulses and emotional triggers, which is why they are more likely to give in to temptations.

The reason behind this difference is still not clear. But there are a lot of ways to increase willpower and improve self-discipline, which will be tackled in the next few chapters.

Why Self-Discipline is important

You already know by now that self-discipline is an important factor in reaching your goals. The Spartans and Special Forces soldiers would not reach that level of success in achieving their goals if they did not practice self-discipline. Sure, it is just one piece of the puzzle, but it is definitely an important piece. It is an essential tool if you want to be successful in life.

For instance, self-discipline played a bigger role when it comes to academic success than IQ. You may be smart and intelligent, but if you do not have the self-discipline to attend classes, submit projects on time, or to study for an exam, you will still get lower grades.

If you are a disciplined and conscientious student who studies every night instead of chatting with friends and watching videos, wakes up early every day and attends classes on time, and finishes projects and submits them before the deadline, you will surely get a higher grade.

Education or attending school is not just about learning new things and acquiring knowledge. It is also about developing your self-discipline to do things that you really do not want to do but you are expected to do to become successful in life.

And when you go out to the real world, your willpower and self-discipline is tested on a daily basis. You might be tempted to stay in bed and call in sick because you do not feel like working. But you still get up and you force yourself to go to work because you need to earn money.

You might be tempted to use your credit card to buy that expensive designer bag that you really, really want. But you don't because you know your salary can't afford it and you don't really need a bag that costs thousands of dollars. Every day you are faced with such temptations and impulses, and every day you fight them. You might get tired, sure, but it is something that you really have to do if you want to achieve your long-term goals, such as saving up for the future.

Moreover, most of the problems that people face in today's world are related to self-discipline or self-control. These include addiction, alcoholism, large debt, unwanted pregnancy, domestic violence, crimes, overeating, sexually transmitted disease, lack of savings, educational failure, under-performance at work, and so on and so forth. The list continues and it's all because people do not have the willpower or self-discipline. This only shows that self-discipline is powerful and should be utilized in order to become a successful individual.

Making the decision to improve your self-discipline is the first step towards success.

This also helps us interact better with other people in society. Just imagine if you do not practice self-discipline. You will just say whatever is on your mind or do whatever you feel like doing without thinking about the consequences of your actions. Rules and regulations in society go hand in hand with discipline. Without these rules and regulations in place, the world will be a dangerous and scary place to live in. And we follow these rules because we have self-discipline.

What does self-discipline look like

It's all talk and mumbo jumbo unless you are given concrete examples of the manifestations of self-discipline in real life. Here are some examples of self-discipline as practiced by ordinary people in different scenarios.

- Emily is a regular employee who works a 9 to 5 office job. She dreams of starting her own business in the future. She does not particularly love her job but it's okay. After all, her job pays her rent and puts food on her table. She wakes up early every day, and writes down ideas and plans for her future business. She goes to work and finishes her workload way before the deadline, which gives her plenty of time to plan more for her business. She receives emails and text messages from shops about their promotion and sales but she ignores them. Instead, she saves up at least 20% of her salary every month and she does not make any unnecessary purchases. Her goal of starting her own business is always in her mind, which makes it easy for her to resist temptations.

- Robert has been drinking since he was a teenager and became a full-blown alcoholic when he got married. He has been having problems with his wife because of this until she decided to leave him, bringing their children with her. He almost lost his job because of his poor performance. One day, he just realized he has had enough and decided to be sober once and for all. He knew he couldn't do it by himself so he asked the help of his best friend. His best friend encouraged him to attend AA meetings so that he can be with other people who are experiencing the same thing. He had to spend to go to these sessions three times a week after work. Whenever he felt like drinking, he would call his friend. It was a difficult journey, but he is now celebrating his 3 years of sobriety. He is also trying to work things out with his wife. One step at a time.

- Victor had been in a car accident and has been in bed for many months. He always felt pain and discomfort. Doctors told him that he would return to his normal, healthy self again, but the process is long and tedious. Some people will feel discouraged and hopeless. But people with enough self-discipline only sees the possibility of being healthy again. Victor still goes to work every day despite the pain and discomfort. He always goes to physical therapy to bring back the strength in his muscles. He also pays close attention to what he eats because he knows that he has to eat only nutritious food. Every day, he makes himself get out of bed, eat breakfast, and go to work because he has a goal in mind—to be healthy again. He does not give in to the temptation of just staying in bed all day because he wants to be better.

- Michelle loves to shop. She loves getting "great deals," and she never misses going to big sales at the malls and her favorite shops. She always maxes out her credit card because she just absolutely had to buy that amazing bag that will go well with her newly-bought outfit or book that ticket to Europe that she barely can afford because all her friends are traveling. She just pays the minimum amount required not to get late fees. But one day, she just realized that she is in too much debt and she has no way of paying it all. She knows she is in big trouble so she decided to make some drastic changes. She researched on ways to pay off credit card debts. She cuts off all her credit cards, and consolidated all her debts in one account. She evaluates her spending habits and finds out that she is spending way more than what she is earning. She decided to let go of things that she does not really need, such as her daily coffee at the Starbucks, dining out or ordering dinner almost every day, and buying unnecessary stuff. She started to list down all her expenses and also her daily expenditures so that she will know where the bulk of her salary goes. She did not develop these habits over time. She did these things one at a time and made sure that she followed her budget to a T every month. How she spent her money before was a perfect example of not having willpower or self-discipline. And how she behaves now is a prime example of someone with strong self-discipline. She hasn't paid off all her debts but she is getting there.

You have also shown self-discipline a lot of times throughout your lifetime but you want to do it like the Spartans and Special Forces did it to get more out of life. The next chapters will let you in on the secret to having a strong willpower and self-discipline. Read on to know more.

3

Developing Self-Discipline

So how do you develop self-discipline? It sounds simple enough, do things that you are supposed to do to reach your goals. What makes it difficult is that these things are not always easy to do. Sometimes, they are even unpleasant tasks. There are also distractions and temptations that prevent you from doing these tasks that sometimes break your willpower.

The process of acquiring self-discipline does not happen overnight. It is not something that you are born with or a talent that comes naturally. It is a long and arduous process that sometimes involves trial and error. You will know what works best for you if you try to do it yourself.

For example, waking up at 5 AM may work for some people, people who are early birds. But if you are a night owl who is most productive when everyone else is sleeping, then by all means stay up late to finish your tasks and sleep until 10 AM. The key here is to find what works best for you. But in general, you can follow the guidelines below to develop your self-discipline. These will work for all kinds of people with different routines and lifestyles.

You need to have a reason why

In short, you need to have a clear goal. What is it that you want to achieve? The sacrifices that you are going to make should be worth it. Your goal is your motivation to overcome these obstacles and stay on track. It is the fuel that self-discipline needs. If you do not have fuel, it will be difficult to go on and continue with the tasks because what's the point? Why do you need to give up that cookie if you do not know why? Why do you need to stop buying clothes if you do not have a goal in mind? Always have a reason for your sacrifices to make them all worthwhile. Otherwise, you will find it difficult to stay focused, especially if you have to do it for a long time.

Your reason should also be compelling enough for you to stick it out until you accomplish it. If you just have a goal for the heck of it, then it might be difficult to stick to your plans. For example, trying to save money just because you want to be able to go out every weekend and meet new people may not be a compelling enough reason to save money. You will just end up telling yourself you can always skip this and just do it online and just continue spending your money buying unnecessary things.

What you can do instead is to find a more worthwhile reason, such as saving up for a house so that you do not have to pay rent and you have a place to live in just in case you decide to start your own family. The more compelling your reason is, the more fuel you will have. The more fuel you have, the stronger your self-discipline will be.

Just take the Spartans as an example. Their fuel was not only compelling, it was a matter of life and death. If they were not strong enough, they would not be granted citizenship and the state would not hesitate to abandon them. The Special Forces also have a compelling reason to always practice self-discipline. They need to complete missions for their country to prevent war or stop terrorism.

What does it take to have self-discipline?

· **Unwavering commitment and accountability**

Self-discipline is not something that you need to do only once. It is a long process that involves several steps, which is why it requires unwavering commitment. This is why it is important that your goal is compelling enough. Otherwise, it would be difficult to stay committed to your plan.

Long-term commitment is challenging, so you need to have some kind of accountability or accountability partner. This way you will be held accountable if you do not stick to your plan and work towards achieving your goal. How do you hold yourself accountable? If you fail to stick to a set schedule, you can punish yourself by working twice as hard the next day or not giving yourself treats and rewards. However, accountability is difficult to achieve if you do it on your own. You can easily tell yourself that you can do it some other day or what harm can a piece of cookie do to your plan to lose weight? You will start fooling yourself that what you are doing is no big deal and you can simply get back on track after this. Before you know it, you are in a lot worse shape than when you started because you just can't help yourself.

If you do not trust yourself, what you need is an accountability partner who will not listen to your excuses and explanations. It can be your spouse or partner, a close friend, or a coworker. Tell your accountability partner your goal and how you are planning to achieve that goal. It would be better if your partner is also trying to reach a goal and improve self-discipline because you can monitor each other's progress. It is amazing how much you can accomplish if you know that someone is going to check on you.

If you remember the Spartan training, the women helped the men to keep in line by humiliating them in public. No wonder they always did their absolute best. You won't get publicly shamed but your friend will know if you are slacking off, which can be a little embarrassing but at the same time can also help keep you on track.

· **Rewards and penalties**

These have been used for decades to foster good behavior. You can also use this to be consistent in the pursuit of your goals. Your levels of motivation can sometimes increase or decrease because of different factors and reasons. There are times when you are just on a roll and you accomplish a lot more than you are supposed to accomplish. If you are in such a momentum, you can reward yourself by simply relaxing for the rest of the day and not doing any chores or tasks.

On the other hand, if you find yourself failing to do what you are supposed to do because you spent your time doing useless things such as watching random videos online or sleeping the whole day, you can penalize yourself by adding more hours to do your tasks that next day or to disconnect from the internet the whole day.

The penalties and rewards are also like fuel to help keep your self-discipline alive and burning until you reach your goal.

· Personal standards

Self-discipline also has a lot to do with one's personal standards. If you set high standards for yourself, you would have better discipline because you are not the type of person to settle for anything less when it comes to how you live your life. These standards are like your personal rules and guidelines that help you when it comes to how you act and make decisions on a daily basis.

One example of a personal standard is to always try to finish major tasks before lunch. This is a higher standard than, say, trying to finish major tasks at the end of office hours. The higher the standard, the more discipline it requires. If you want to improve your self-discipline and the overall quality of your life, you have to raise the bar and set high personal standards. It is like striking a deal with one's self. You have a list of things that you will allow yourself to do and things that you won't. These guidelines will serve as the cornerstone of your self-discipline. Basically, self-discipline is like regulating your decisions, behaviors, and actions and correcting mistakes if you find yourself getting off track.

· Competitive environment

If what you are doing feels like a competition, you will most likely achieve your goals because you know that there are a winner and a loser and you definitely do not want to be the loser. There are two ways to look at this.

First, you can compete against other people. You can ask your accountability partner who is also trying to achieve the same goal if you can do it like a competition between the two of you. If you don't have a partner, you can compete against people who are doing the same thing even without telling them. For instance, you and your coworker are doing the same project with the same deadline. You can tell yourself that you have to finish it before your coworker without really telling him or her what you are doing. Just keep the competition to yourself.

The second way to create a competitive environment is to compete against yourself—more specifically, against your "best self". Always look back on what you have accomplished and try to surpass it. For example, if you were able to finish a specific task within two hours, try to do it within a shorter period of time, say, an hour. Push yourself towards excellence and create the very best version of yourself.

- **Supportive environment**

Your environment or the place you are working or doing your tasks should also be considered. You may have the right mindset but if your environment is not conducive to self-discipline, then it will make things a lot more difficult. There will be more temptations, and controlling yourself will be a tougher task. For example, if you are trying to finish some work at home, you should have a room or at least a space in your house that you can use for working. Working on your bed is not a good idea because it would be too tempting to tell yourself that you are just going to lie down for a minute to rest your eyes. Before you know it, it's already morning and you weren't able to finish anything.

Or if you are trying to save money, try not to go to the mall or browse online unless you absolutely need to buy something. This keeps you from splurging on things that you can't really afford and you don't really need. If you are trying to lose weight and you live with other people, tell them that you are trying to lose weight. If they care about you, they will try not to eat chocolates or cakes in front of you. Or if you cannot tell them because you are not really close, just try to go out of the house or go to your room when they are eating.

It all boils down to making yourself more comfortable as much as you can while you are doing the tasks that you need to do and removing temptations. Creating a supportive environment is something that should be done if you really want to be self-disciplined at all times.

Steps to develop self-discipline

· **Set clear goals**

As stated previously, you need to set clear goals that you want to achieve. Imagine yourself as an archer. Your target is your goal. It is hard to be disciplined if you do not even know what you want. Your goal can be any kind of positive change in your life. Maybe you want to learn something new, like a new language. Or maybe you want to develop a new habit, like eating balanced meals every day. You can also change a behavior that you have which you think does not make you a better person, such as gossiping about other people. Anything can be a goal but make sure that it is something that you really desire and will contribute to a better you and a better life for yourself.

· *Make priorities*

Making a list of the things that you need to do before you go to bed and prioritizing the things that are most important is a great way to develop self-discipline. It may seem like a cliché but writing them down on paper and ticking them one by one as you finish each task is fulfilling, especially when you cross out the last item on your list. The most important ones and the ones with the shortest deadlines should be at the top of the list. Try to tackle difficult tasks first when your brain is still fresh. Moreover, taking the largest burden off your mind will make it easier for you to finish the rest of the tasks on your list. You do not want to waste your peak energy level on tasks that are not really that

important.

· **Know yourself**

It is easier to practice self-discipline if you know yourself and you know what will work for you. As mentioned earlier, if you know you are a night owl and you work better at night, do not force yourself to wake up early in the morning. If you know you get easily tempted when you browse online shops, remove the temptation by not browsing online or at least keeping your credit card somewhere out of reach. Some even go as far as submerging their credit card in water and putting it inside the freezer just so they will have a hard time reaching for it when they feel the urge to buy.

There may also be tasks that you do not have to include in your suffering and will not in any way affect your planned timeline of reaching your goals. If you want to stop smoking cigarettes, you do not necessarily have to stop going out with friends who smoke because that will not in any way affect your goal. You can stop smoking in other ways by not buying cigarettes in the first place or not joining them when they go for a cigarette break.

Also keep in mind that the basic idea behind self-discipline is overcoming suffering and pain. You need to know your pain tolerance. You should also understand that it's not just suffering that is necessary to achieve your goals. You have to be honest with yourself and understand your limits. You can maybe push yourself but do it little by little so that you won't feel that all you do is suffer and sacrifice.

· **Visualize**

Another thing that you should do to develop self-discipline is visualizing the positive results of not giving in to impulses and instant rewards. Imagine yourself owning your own house and living comfortably after retirement if you are trying to save for the future. Imagine yourself looking amazing and healthy a year from now if you are planning to lose weight. Imagine yourself having more free time during the day if you decide to tackle your tasks right away.

The Spartans visualized becoming citizens, starting their own family, and serving their beloved state. The Special Operations soldiers also visualized accomplishing important missions that will put their names or at least their troops in history books. Visualizing your long-term reward will help keep you going. Your visualization can serve as your motivation to not give up and not give in whenever you feel the urge or the impulse to do things that you are not supposed to be doing.

Be mindful of your choices

Developing self-discipline is also about making the right choices. You need to recognize your power to choose in every aspect of your life. Every single choice and decision that you make will contribute to how you can achieve your goals. When you wake to the sound of your alarm in the morning, you have the power to choose to ignore it and press snooze and continue sleeping, or to get up right away and start your day early. If you understand how powerful your choices are in creating the path towards your goal, then you will be more mindful of your choices. The path to your goals may be difficult but it is definitely a lot shorter. Self-discipline will always guide you to the right choice that will lead you to the right path to achieve your objectives in life.

Make it a habit

Self-discipline involves making changes in your normal day-to-day routine. And making changes, especially in the beginning, can feel awkward and uncomfortable. Here is the explanation why. The part of the brain involved in habitual or repetitive behaviors that you sometimes do on autopilot is the basal ganglia. It recognizes patterns and memories. On the other hand, active decision-making happens in the pre-frontal cortex, where the process of self-discipline also takes place.

Any new decision that you make will feel uncomfortable and "not right" at first because it is new and it is still in the prefrontal cortex. But when you do it on a regular basis and you form a habit out of it, that behavior will then move to the basal ganglia, which does not require effort because you do it without thinking, like your habits.

This is why you should not wait for it to feel right because it will not feel right unless you make it happen. Breaking a bad habit and starting a new habit at first will feel wrong, wrong in the sense that it will feel like you are exerting too much effort doing it, such as getting up early in the morning when your alarm goes off. But when you continue doing it every day, your brain and body will get used to it, and the brain will recognize the behavior as a habit, something that it is programmed to do. So embrace that wrong and difficult feeling that your new habit is giving you, because it will feel right once it becomes a part of your normal routine.

These are just some of the things that you can do to develop self-discipline. You can tweak the steps a little bit or add more based on your own experiences as you continue towards your journey of becoming a more disciplined individual like the Spartans and soldiers of the Special Operations Units.

4

Self-Discipline and Freedom

Self-discipline and freedom are two words that you do not often associate with each other. When you hear the word self-discipline, you automatically think balls and chains or limiting the things that you can do and sacrificing a lot of things. Sure, it helps you achieve your goals but practicing self-discipline is not exactly a walk in the park and it sometimes involves giving up things that you like doing but are detrimental to your life goals. For some people, self-discipline is like a master that has a whip in his hand that makes you do tasks that you really don't want to do.

Words that you associate with self-discipline are limitation, control, and restraint. So how is it associated with freedom? When freedom is all about allowance, flexibility, and some might even say indulgence. The truth is that self-discipline brings you freedom—freedom to do things that you like. It is impossible to experience the power and benefits of freedom if you do not practice self-discipline. Moreover, you have to understand that freedom always comes with responsibility, and that's where self-discipline enters the picture.

Imagine how hard the Spartans had to train, which involved strict discipline, for them to be able to become citizens who had the privilege to marry, vote, and run for office. The elite Special Forces also follow a lot of standard operational procedures. It may seem overly cautious to an outsider, but it actually makes things more efficient.

Following regulations lead to shorter and faster processes, which means freeing up time that the soldiers can spend to finish other tasks or maybe to take a break. The more structured and stricter the procedures are, the more freedom the troop has to operate at a more efficient rate because the soldiers know and understand what is expected of them. It is an interesting paradox, how structure results in liberation.

This is also how democracy should work. A democratic country can only fully experience the benefits and power of freedom if the people practice discipline. In a larger context, discipline is equivalent to the laws of that country. If people do not follow a set of rules and regulations, there would be chaos because people can just do whatever they want. Freedom without discipline is not good and can only result in excessiveness. This is why these two concepts go hand in hand.

Self-discipline is the giver of freedom. It does not take away freedom to do things, as most people believe. It is, in fact, the opposite because it gives you the power to be the person you really want to be by helping you achieve your life goals.

Stop thinking about the things that you cannot do or the things that you are not allowed to do because it is just one aspect of self-discipline. And most of these things are things that you cannot do at the moment but you can do later when you are done doing more important tasks. Unless, of course, it is a bad habit, which is something that you have to give up for good. Do not think that discipline limits the things that you can do when in fact it gives you even more freedom to do other things.

If you want concrete examples of how self-discipline can give you freedom, check out the next few paragraphs.

Scenario #1

Putting things back to where they belong after using them is a form of discipline. You hear your mom always say this to you when you were younger, and later on your spouse after getting married. It is something that many people have been taught to do but still fail to do it. For example, putting the scissors back into the drawer or your keys to the hook on your wall is something that you always do.

The freedom that comes with it is that you do not need to waste time and energy searching for the scissors or keys because you know where you put them. And they are always there no matter how many times you use them because you always put them to their respective places. By simply putting things back where they belong, which only takes a few seconds of your life, you free up minutes of your life that you would have spent searching for the missing things if you did not put them in their right places.

Scenario #2

You make it a point to wake up early every day at exactly six in the morning. Sure, you find it difficult to do the first few days and also during winter when your bed feels a lot warmer and more inviting. But as you continuously do it, you become used to it and it is now a part of your habit.

The reward? You get to finish your tasks early which gives you plenty of free time to spend with your family without worrying about tasks that you have not yet finished. If you wake up early in the morning to go to the gym before you go to work, you can simply relax when you reach home and not force yourself to go to the gym, which can be too tiring especially after a long day of work. By starting your day early, you also finish your day early, which gives you plenty of free time before going to bed to simply unwind and relax.

Scenario #3

You are going on vacation and your flight is tomorrow. You still have one week to prepare. You prepared a list of things to do and to bring such as your tickets, passport, clothes, toiletries, and so on. You bought all the things that you don't have at home but you need to bring on your trip. You packed your bags and made sure that everything on your list is crossed out. You also made sure that you washed all your dirty clothes before you leave. You cleaned up the house and brought out the trash.

On the day of your trip, you feel relaxed and you have everything you need in your bags. You arrived on time at the airport and checked in without a hassle. When you returned home, you only have to unpack your bags and wash dirty clothes from your trip because you didn't leave any chores unfinished before you left for vacation. Everything went smoothly from the time you left to the time you return home and you were able to relax on your well-deserved vacation.

Scenario #4

You try to save up money by not buying things that you do not really need. You used to always go to the mall and hunt for sales—clothes, bags, shoes, home decors—you name it. But you decide to just stop it because it is bad for your bank account and you are trying to save up on something that you have been really wanting to do—visit Spain. Besides, you don't really like the things that you used to buy. You just buy them because they are on sale.

Now, you are wiser. You also stopped ordering for lunch and instead you bring your own lunch to work every day, which saves you a lot of money. All you have to do is plan and prepare your meals for the whole week over the weekend and you do not need to think of what to cook every day, which can be stressful. You also stopped going to Starbucks every day because their coffee is expensive. You still go there from time to time but not as often as before.

Finally, after months of saving, you now have the freedom to go to your dream destination. You have no worries because you have the money to pay for everything. You did not even need to use your credit card. Everything is paid for in cash so that when you return from your vacation, you do not have to worry about paying off your bills. Saving up money means practicing self-discipline by limiting your purchases to be able to do something that you really want to do. It also gives you financial freedom during your vacation because you prepared for it and you saved up for it. Plus, you did not incur debt by not using your credit card.

5

Building Mental Toughness

You have probably wondered what makes people great at what they do. Why are there great athletes, leaders, students, artists, and so on? What separates greatness from mediocrity? What do they have that others don't? Some might say these people are more talented or more intelligent; that's why they are able to achieve their goals consistently. But the truth is, intelligence or talent is not the only answer. In fact, according to studies, intelligence or talent only accounts for 30% of a person's success. It takes a lot more than that.

So what makes these people successful? The answer is mental toughness, or what others call *grit*. And what's great about it is that it can be learned. It is not something that you are born with, like intelligence or talent. So why is it important in achieving success? Let's discuss it a little bit more.

Mental toughness of soldiers

Soldiers are known not only for their physical strength but also for their mental toughness. For instance, the United States Military Academy cadets have to undergo a number of tests and initiations to know how far they can go physically and mentally. And you probably think that the people who succeed in these brutal tests are the biggest, strongest, and most intelligent cadets. Being big and strong and intelligent sure does help a lot but what's even more useful is the person's perseverance, resilience, and passion in what he does.

You may be strong and intelligent but if your mind already gave up, then there is really nothing you can do about it. Your mental strength is the trait that will push you to the finish line, not intelligence or strength, especially if it is a long and arduous test.

This is what the Spartans and the Special Forces soldiers have in common—they have the mental toughness that allow them to endure any physical, emotional, and mental hardships that they had to undergo to be able to become worthy Spartans or Special Forces soldiers.

Who exhibits mental toughness?

Aside from the Spartans, Delta Force, SAS, Navy SEALS, and other Special Operations Units, other groups of people also show mental toughness. These are people who excel at what they do. For example, it may be difficult to get into an Ivy League school but getting in is a lot easier than staying. This is because you need mental toughness or grit to be able to maintain a high GPA while inside the school.

People who join contests such as the National Spelling Bee contests are not necessarily the most intelligent students in their class. They are most often the ones who show grit and who are committed to spend hours to study new words and practice a couple of hours every day. You may be a talented writer but to be able to become a successful writer, you have to spend several hours a day not only writing but also reading books, which takes mental toughness.

Successful athletes also have to undergo intensive training and practice. Kobe Bryant, Cristiano Ronaldo, and Roger Federer didn't get to where they are right now solely because of talent. Actors and actresses who are excellent at their craft also have a lot of grit in them. They have to study their characters deeply, memorize scripts, and go to shooting schedules at the wee hours of the day.

Regular people employees also show mental toughness on a daily basis. These are the employees who finish their tasks on or before the set deadline. They are also highly reliable because their bosses know that they will not slack off.

Look around you every day and you will see people showing mental toughness. You probably even have exhibited mental toughness before when you forced yourself to finish something that you have to do even when temptations surround you. You didn't give in and you didn't give up no matter what until you achieved what you have to do. It is accepting discomfort for the sake of reaching your goal. That's mental toughness for you.

Daily practices for mental toughness

Like the Spartans and the Special Operations Units, you also need to experience discomfort that will improve your mental toughness. There are practices that you can incorporate in your daily routine that will help improve your mental toughness and will in turn develop your self-discipline. Here are some of them.

1 .Take cold showers

Did you know that the Spartans bathed in ice-cold water on a daily basis because "comfort zone" was not a part of their vocabulary? In fact, this is technique is also done by world-class athletes because of how effective it is in improving their mental toughness. They take a cold shower for as long as 30 minutes! You might think this is an unnecessary suffering but it is not because taking cold showers has a lot of benefits such as boosting your immune system, increasing levels of testosterone, reducing inflammation, and so on. When the cold water touches your skin for the first time, try not to yell or wince. Just bear it and keep your mind and body as relaxed as possible by taking deep breaths. Try to stay in the cold water for at least 30 seconds and just make it longer as you get used to the coldness.

2.Minimize social media usage

What do you need social media for, anyway, aside from sharing memes and other unimportant stuff? Moreover, you just sometimes get negative feelings such as envy, irritation, insecurity, and so on when you log in to your numerous social media accounts. People become addicted to it because it is like crack. It gives you that unnatural high with every like, comment, and notification that you get. When you scroll through your newsfeed, you will most likely click on a post that catches your attention, you will read it and before you know it, you are on your tenth post and reading comments of people you don't really know about something that you don't really care about. It's a waste of time.

It takes a lot of mental toughness to unplug from social media. You can either stop using it completely or try to use it only when necessary, like for communication or sharing important stuff. But minimize social media usage as much as you can and just spend your free time doing more productive things. Believe it or not, Steve Jobs didn't let his kids use iPads because he knew how toxic it can get once people start to go online and use social media.

3.Get out of bed right away

When you hear your alarm go off in the morning, do not press snooze and do not stay in your bed even for just one minute longer. Jump out of bed when you wake up in the morning and do not tell yourself "ten more minutes" or "I'll just rest my eyes" because let's not fool ourselves here. People who say these things and do them usually end up getting up a lot later that their intended time. Get out of bed right away and do something to keep your blood flowing. Splash your face with cold water, make coffee or tea, prepare breakfast, and just do anything to wake yourself up. This is all just mind over matter. And you will feel a lot better later on when you realize how much you were able to finish in a day because you woke up early.

4.Sleep on the floor

You can also try sleeping on the floor once in a while. You don't necessarily need to give up your comfortable bed for good. Just do this from time to time to help you build your mental toughness. For a really tough challenge, sleep without a blanket. Use a thin sheet if you are not ready for the more challenging level. Do you think the Spartans and Special Forces slept on a soft bed with fluffy pillows and warm blanket? If they did, they'd probably still wake up really early for their drills. But they surely didn't have this luxury. So if you want to be just like them, try to experience this once in a while. Believe me, this will make you appreciate your bed and pillows and blanket a lot more than you used to.

5.Do small exercises

This will not be your regular full-blown workout. That is another thing that you should be doing even if you are not trying to lose weight because it will keep your body strong and healthy. These mini workouts are those workouts that you can incorporate in your everyday life. This is especially helpful if you work in a 9 to 5 job sitting in front of the computer the whole day. Try to do a set of 25 to 50 squats, sit-ups, push-ups, jumping jacks, or any other form of exercise that you can do in your office. Try to do this at least every hour, or depending on how much your office will allow you to take a break during office hours. Instead of going for a cigarette break or to the pantry to have snacks, get out of your comfort zone and instead do some exercises that will keep you from being completely sedentary.

6.Move slowly

You might think that this tip is counter intuitive because slowness is often not associated with success and achieving goals. But this does not literally mean working at a slower pace. It just means that you do not make impulsive actions and snap decisions. For example, when you go to your car, open the door, and sit in the driver's seat, what's the first thing you do? You probably connect your phone to the car stereo to play some of your favorite songs. Why not consider doing it deliberately by not rushing? It is being mindful of every move and decision you make. If you are not impulsive and you are deliberate at everything you do, you will keep yourself from making mistakes and wrong decisions. By moving in a more deliberate style, you are teaching yourself to be more in control of your actions. You will take more time to react to thoughts and emotions and also to make important decisions.

7.Get dirty

Some people are so afraid to get themselves dirty because getting dirty is way out of their comfort zone. Although being clean is something that we should all strive for, there is nothing wrong with getting yourself dirty from time to time. NOTE: If you are already a slob, then you should skip this tip or consider doing the reverse—get yourself cleaned up. Try to walk inside your house or in your front yard with bare feet. If a piece of food like a chip or cookie falls on the floor, do not be afraid to pick it up and eat it. Squish bugs such as mosquitoes using your bare hands. Try not to take a shower at least once a week (unless you have just been working out and you were sweating heavily). Just basically try not to be comfortably clean from time to time. Did you know that the Spartans and Special Operations Unit sometimes go for days or weeks without showering especially when they are in the middle of combat? Try to do this yourself and see how much your mental toughness will improve.

8.Read

Reading a book can make you tougher mentally because it helps you improve your mental focus for a long period of time. Read a book for a couple of hours every day that can teach you a thing or two about delayed gratification, unlike the television and online videos that are considered passive entertainment and do not really contribute anything to improving your mental toughness. Reading is also an activity that allows you to actively use your mind, and learning new words and information is always a welcome bonus.

Four mental toughness techniques inspired by war

War is never a good thing but you got to do what you got to do so just make the most of the situation by finding the silver lining, such as learning some life lessons from it. You already know by now that the epitome of mental toughness is the Special Operations Units or the Spartans. Both are, without a doubt, mentally tough. And they have to be mentally tough, apart from also being physically and emotionally strong, in preparation for war. So what mental toughness techniques inspired by war that you can try in your day-to-day life?

Check out the following:

1.Train to increase confidence

The training of the Spartans and the Special Forces are repetitive—they have to do things over and over again until they master the task. And isn't this how practice and training works? You repeatedly do things until you become good at it. And when you are good at something, it gives you a boost of confidence.

The number one goal of the Special Forces is to achieve the mission, whatever it is. The protection of the members of the troop only comes in second. It is safe to say that completing the mission is more important than the safety of the soldiers. Leaders and commanders have no other choice but to send their team into combat for them to achieve the goal. It is a must in any war. And as a leader, you have to show confidence in your decision to send out troops who could get killed while doing their duty. Whether you are leading five or five hundred people, you need to project 100% confidence because they also get their confidence from their leaders.

Aggressive training for confidence for the soldiers also applies for ordinary people who want to improve their mental toughness. What you can do is to start practicing steadily and deliberately. Try to overcome small obstacles first to slowly gain confidence before you tackle bigger challenges in your life.

As an exercise, think of something that you badly want to do but you do not know how to do it well, for instance, playing the guitar. Consider it as your little petri dish, or experiment. Every day, do some exercises or activities that will make you improve your guitar-playing skills, such as playing short and simple pieces then later on moving to more difficult ones. You will gain confidence as you learn the skill over time that will give you mental toughness to endure anything that will keep you from reaching your goals.

2.Develop your sense of duty

Sometimes, it is more effective to simply tell yourself that "it's your job" for you to finish what you need to do. It is the simplest and easiest form of mental toughness. Soldiers train and practice because they know that it is their job. Their job is to fight for their country and protect their countrymen against their enemies. And also, they benefit personally, such as earning a monthly salary or in the case of the Spartans, becoming a citizen. If you understand your responsibilities and you know the consequences of not doing them, it will be much easier to finish tasks.

As an exercise, write down all your responsibilities for the different roles you play in life—employee, parent, partner, etc. Tape your list somewhere you can easily see and tweak them every week. Your responsibilities are your duties—duties to your employers, to your loved ones, and also to yourself. It may not be a matter of life and death but a lot of people still depend on you. And it is a man's duty to finish what he has started and to do the things that he had agreed to do because a man keeps his word.

3.Do it for your troop

The idea behind the military will not work if the members do not have teamwork. In fact, they train soldiers to remove any sense of individualism when inside the barracks and when they do their job. This is because someone who is too individualistic may end up not following orders of the commander and can be disastrous in any operation. People who care more about themselves than about the team will also save their behind's first than look after their team members, something that is highly discouraged in the military. In fact, the Marines has a saying that "No one gets left behind", whether that soldier is alive or already died or is beyond help. Everyone has to be saved.

The point here is that it is important to have a strong group of people around you who will support you no matter what and vice versa. You do not need to die for them. It can be something like being there for each other when one member of the family is fighting a serious illness, trying to keep your company afloat with your team, or when you just lost your job and you need to start searching for a new one—situations like these can make or break a man. But if you have the right group of people around you, then you will surely overcome such challenges and will therefore increase your mental toughness.

For your exercise, make a list of all the people whom you trust and you know you can depend on. Strengthen your relationship with these people and let go of people in your life who do nothing but let you down or make you feel worthless. You will be more likely to succeed and overcome big challenges in life if you are surrounded with these positive people.

4. Take pride in what you do

Awards and rewards for a job well done are helpful when it comes to boosting someone's morale and motivation. But what's even more important than any trophy or medal is how you feel inside. Taking pride in what you do and your accomplishments is already a kind of reward in itself. Soldiers in combat do incredible and amazing things on a daily basis and they do not receive special awards for them. And this is not done intentionally by the government because they try to recognize these soldiers' achievements as much as they can. But of course, not everything is noticed and recorded and most of these soldiers just keep their accomplishments to themselves, not wanting any of the recognition because it already gave them a feeling of pride. And for them, that's enough.

In your life, just because you do not get recognition for something that you do does not mean you have to stop doing it. Keep on doing what you need to do not to get awards but to take pride in yourself. And once you take pride in what you do, you will become mentally tougher because your resilience to endure does not only come from the outside but more importantly from the inside.

6

.

Improving Focus and Concentration

Another important characteristic of the Spartans and Special Operations Units is their ability to focus no matter where they are and what they are doing.

Most of their missions require high concentration and focus. The opposite can prove dangerous and fatal. Snipers have to focus on their target if they want a sure hit.

Soldiers have to be alert at all times during combat to know if enemies are coming. People who are scatterbrained and who always find themselves daydreaming have no room in such kinds of missions. They will just put themselves and their team's lives in danger and also jeopardize the operation. This can cost a lot of time, resources, and lives.

Some people think that the most difficult part of a sniper's job is to successfully shoot the target from afar but there's a lot more to a sniper's job than this. In fact, what's even more difficult for them is to go to a dangerous area, like the enemy's lair, to collect surveillance, and be as invisible and silent as possible.

Being seen or heard by the enemy is fatal, which makes it a lot more difficult than simply sitting somewhere far from the target and trying to find the right angle to shoot. Being invisible and silent is extremely difficult especially if you are a hulking man carrying gear and equipment. Add the fact that you also feel hungry, thirsty, tired, and sleepy, every aching muscle and bone in your body screaming for rest. It is easy to lose focus with all these distractions and challenges, but a great soldier never loses focus and keeps moving until he completes his task.

Your challenges in life may not be a matter of life or death but you can apply the same techniques that these elite soldiers are using to improve their mental focus and concentration.

What is focus?

First, you need to know what focus means. It is the act of concentrating all your attention on something, whether it is an object, an activity, a task, an event, and so on. The definition may seem boring to you but there is more to focus than simply concentrating on one thing. More often than not, several different things sometimes try to get your attention, and this is what makes you lose focus on what you are doing. So aside from concentrating on one thing, focusing is also the act of ignoring other things, which sounds easier said than done.

Eliminating other factors that will divide your attention is an important prerequisite of focus. You have to say yes to only one thing, and no to the rest so that one thing will have your full and undivided attention. Saying no to those other things is not permanent. It is just saying no to doing those things at that particular instant. To be productive, you need to have focus. Focus on the things that matter and eliminate the distractions. You also have to prioritize the things that you need to focus on.

Here are some steps that you can try to improve your focus.

Stop, look, listen, and smell

When you find yourself distracted from fatigue, hunger, and the difficulty of your task, you need to shift your focus and attention from your mission and try to take a short break by doing SLLS. You should stop what you are doing in the moment, look all around you, listen to any small movement, and smell your surroundings. The main objective of taking an SLLS break is to refocus and also take a much-needed break, albeit a short one. This will at least keep you mindful of your surroundings and will help you focus on your mission.

This is also helpful in an office setting when you find yourself bombarded by emails that you feel you should respond to right away and the hundred and one tasks that your boss wants you to do. Try to refocus by doing SLLS. This is especially helpful if you have a lot of things in mind and a lot of tasks to finish within the same deadline. It will help keep your mind focused on what needs to be done instead of it jumping from one external stimulus to another, such as your coworker's ringing phone, the pinging of your email notification, the smell of someone's lunch heating in the microwave, the high pile of papers on your desk, and many other things that can get you distracted.

Stop whatever it is you are doing, look around you and try to organize the piles of paper on your desk, listen to the ringing phone of your coworker until he picks it up, and simply enjoy the smell of the food. Sometimes, all you need is to be mindful of the things around you instead of simply reacting to them impulsively and negatively. Just take it all in especially if there is really nothing you can do about them. Just make them a part of your groove.

Situational awareness

The Special Forces Units are taught a technique called situational awareness. It is defined as the ability to understand important factors and elements of the current situation of the troop in relation to their mission. In short, being aware of your surroundings and what's happening around you.

During combat, situational awareness is crucial because it can help you save lives. People today are not often aware of their surroundings. When you go to the airport or a shopping mall, do you think these people are aware of their surroundings? Probably not. They just go about their lives, inside their little bubble, not caring about what's going on around them.

You can improve your focus by doing these situational awareness exercises. This is more effective if you do it in a large, crowded place, like the mall, airport, stadium, or any place where people seem to just not care about their surroundings. These exercises will help boost your concentration and focus.

· Take note of the things that the people around you are doing
· Try to guess what they are thinking and why they are in that place

· Look for behaviors, actions, or things that you find odd or out of place

Doing these exercises will help improve your focus and will also make you pay closer attention to small details. This is something that you can use wherever you are to be able to successfully achieve your goals.

Breathe properly

Another technique that you can do to keep your focus is to learn how to breathe properly for relieving stress and tension. When you have so much stuff to do and you feel overwhelmed by it all, you should take deep breaths to gather your wits and stay focused. When you feel your body becoming taut and tight and you notice that your breaths are faster and shallower, you are under a lot of stress and tension so try to release it by breathing properly.

By taking control of your breathing, you feel calmer and more relaxed. Start by sitting up straight with your shoulders relaxed and your hands on your lap. Empty your lungs by exhaling deeply. Fill your lungs by inhaling slowly and deeply. Count to four as you take a deep breath. Hold your breath for four seconds, then exhale slowly again for four seconds. Repeat the whole process ten times. Be sure to inhale through your nose and exhale through your mouth.

Different Special Forces Units use this technique to stay calm and focused and they call it the four-box breathing technique. The situations they are in are a lot more stressful than what ordinary people usually face on a daily bases but it works for them, which means that it will definitely work for you.

Another breathing technique that you can try is to take three deep breaths, making sure that each breath is slower and deeper than the previous one. As you slowly inhale and exhale, make sure that all your muscles are relaxed, especially your tongue, jaw, and forehead. You probably don't notice it but when you feel stressed and therefore out of focus, your forehead is wrinkled, your jaw is tight, and your tongue is stuck to the roof of your mouth. Just breathe deeply and feel all your muscles relax. You can also wiggle your toes or bend your knees a bit to further keep your body relaxed.

Have a distraction to-do list

Oftentimes, you find yourself thinking about something else while you are working on something. For example, you are finishing a report about your company's monthly sales. And sometimes, things just pop in your head, whether they are related to what you are working on or not. It is easy to fall into the trap of googling the question right so that you will have the answer right away but this will steer you away from what you are doing.

What you can do instead is to create a distraction to-do list where you can write down all the things that crossed your mind while working and then research about them later after you finish your tasks. Questions like, "what will be the weather tomorrow", "who's that actor who starred in that movie I watched last night", "what is the title of that song", and so on. Write all of these down and get back to them later when you have free time. But first, finish your task at hand.

Meditate

Meditation does not only make you feel calm and collected and help you keep your cool in stressful situations. It also helps increase your attention span which in turn improves your focus. The longer your attention span, the longer you will be able to focus on your tasks. You do not need to spend all day meditating like monks in a monastery. You can try simple meditation techniques such as the breathing technique mentioned earlier and other tricks that can help improve you focus. This will only take a few minutes every day and you do not even need a special place to do it.

Control the voice in your head

Sometimes, the distractions are all in your head. You hear that small voice in your head that gives criticisms or distracts you from finishing your tasks. Try to control this voice and do not let it ruin your momentum, especially if it is trying to bring you down and make you feel bad about yourself or if it is trying to distract you from your task. Try to ignore this voice especially when you find yourself second-guessing your decisions and actions. If you find yourself in this predicament, just pay attention to what you are doing and try to focus on the rewards if you finish your task on time.

Another thing that you can do is to go over every little detail and every angle of your decision or task and try to find loopholes that will make it easier for that inner critic to plant seeds of doubts in your head. By understanding what needs to be done and what actions you can take in different scenarios, you will have a strong defense against your inner critic because you know what you are doing.

Focus on one thing at a time

Nowadays, companies sing the praises of people who are efficient multitaskers. In fact, it is included in the list of traits that they are looking for in their job applicants when they post job vacancies. But is multitasking really better than focusing on one single thing? The answer is that multitasking is better used in mundane tasks, or tasks that do not involve deep thinking, such as talking on the phone, replying to a regular email, and printing a document. Things like these do not require you to think.

However, when it comes to finishing a task that requires your full attention, you need to focus on it alone without doing ten other different things at the same time. For example, finishing that novel that you started, creating a design for your company's website, learning how to play the piano, and so on. If you want to master any skill, you need to give it your 100% undivided attention while you are doing it.

Moreover, multitasking can lead to more mistakes than doing one task at a time because your attention is divided. To illustrate this more clearly, imagine your attention as a spotlight. If the spotlight is focused on one spot only, without moving, then you will clearly see all the details in that area. You can give more details and your description is more accurate. But if you have to move the spotlight several times in different areas, you will only catch a short glimpse of each area. Your descriptions of each area will not be as detailed and accurate because your time and resources are divided into different things.

So be sure to use your attention wisely and try to use it on things that really matter.

Practice pre-commitment

Pre-commitment is a fancier word for your to-do list. This is the act of deciding in advance what project you are going to finish first before you start working on the others and for how long you are going to work on that project. This will help you to focus more on one task because you know what needs to be done and you have a deadline for yourself.

For example, if it is a weekend, you can start working on a difficult task first, such as working out for a full hour. You can then tackle other easier tasks such as decluttering, cleaning the house, doing the laundry, washing the dishes, and so on. You can probably schedule your whole Saturday doing house chores after you finish working out so that these tasks are already out of the way and you can spend your whole Sunday just relaxing or hanging out with your family or friends. Setting a deadline for each task will also keep you from dawdling on one task and just concentrate on finishing it before the deadline.

Pay attention to the process

More often than not, people pay more attention to the end-result and just pay little attention to the process. Success is not a one-time event because it involves a lot of process along the way. It is not just a single event of losing 20 pounds in six months, getting your novel published, or achieving your target sales. It also involves your commitment to the whole process or journey of achieving that result. People who are successful in what they do fall in love with the process, and the positive results is the icing on top.

For example, to become a published writer, your main goal is to get published of course but you have to fall in love with the tedious process of writing and editing and researching if you want to achieve your goal. If your goal is to lose weight, you have to fall in love with keeping in shape by eating healthy food and going to the gym. Success and rewards are just the tip of the iceberg and this is what people often see. They fail to realize that there is a lot more underneath, which includes perseverance, hard-work, discipline, and many other things that contribute to a person's success.

7

Forming Good Habits and Breaking Bad Habits

You are all too familiar with the word 'habit'. You use it in your normal conversation and you understand what it means. You can call them a behavior pattern, a routine, or anything that you do repeatedly, either consciously or unconsciously. Your day will not be complete without your habit because it is a part of your day-to-day routine.

How do habits work? Habits are learned behavior, meaning you are not born with them, you acquire them from somewhere. The whole process starts with a cue or a trigger. This can be in the form of time, location, thought, emotion, people, belief, or behavior. After the trigger comes the craving, which is the motivation or desire for the action. This is then followed by the action itself or your response to the craving. After performing the action, you get the reward that you are expecting, and this reward is what drives you to perform the action repeatedly.

Let's illustrate the process of habit so that you will understand it better. Let's say for example your habit is to drink coffee when you wake up. Your trigger is waking up in the morning. You drink coffee because you want to feel awake and alert, which is your craving. Then your response is to drink coffee. Your reward is you feel alert after drinking coffee. Another example is biting your nails, which is a form of bad habit. The trigger is stress at work. Craving is your need to feel calm and in control. Your response is to bite your nails. Your reward is that you feel calmer and more in control while biting your nails.

The Spartans and the Special Operations Units have good habits that contribute to their excellent performance. Their habits are so ingrained in their system that they do these behaviors even when they are no longer in the military. Take the retired soldiers, for example. Waking up really early in the morning, getting a crew cut instead of a stylish hairdo, eating fast and without wastage, and living in simplicity and austerity are habits that they carry with them even after retirement.

There are two kinds of habits—good habits and bad habits. Of course, you want to continue doing your good habits and maybe learn some new ones. And you want to break your bad habits and replace them with good ones.

Forming good habits

1.Start small

To prevent yourself from feeling overwhelmed with what you want to achieve, you need to start small. For instance, if your main goal is to have a healthier lifestyle, going from 0 to five times a week of gym workouts or switching to a vegan diet from a diet loaded with carbs and meat may be too difficult to accomplish. This can cause a problem later on because you might not stick to doing your good habit for a long time because you feel like you are sacrificing a lot. This is why it is important to start small.

Maybe try to go to the gym during weekends and cut back on your carbs and sweets first. When you get used to this, try to tweak it a little bit and make it more challenging by going to the gym four times a week and reducing your meat intake. By slowly easing yourself into the habit, it will feel natural and normal, as if it has been a part of your routine for a long time.

2.Make your intentions clear

You need to be clear and specific about what you want to achieve if you are really serious about forming a new habit. if you plan out the details of your habit, you will most likely follow through to the end.

The first thing that you can do is to create a schedule or deadline for your habit. If it is important for you, you will surely make time for it. If your schedule is packed throughout the day and you really cannot change anything, why not wake up a little earlier so that you have time to do your new habit, especially if it is something important.

Another technique that you can try to make your intentions clear is habit stacking. This is linking your new habit to an existing habit that is already a part of your routine. You can say "Before going to bed, I will read a book for at least 30 minutes". By linking the new habit to an old habit, it is easier for you to remember doing it and it will become like a continuation of your old habit.

You can also try the implementation intention, wherein you consider your habit a conditional action. You can say something like "If I wake up at 6AM, then I will do ten pushups."

3.Get hooked

Have you ever been so engrossed in a book that you finish it in just one night? Have you started a project that you really like doing and you find it difficult to stop working on it? This is the same with habits. You form habits because you get hooked on doing them. So make sure that you find a way to get hooked on doing your habit.

One technique that you can try is the "don't break the chain" technique. Whenever you finish doing the habit for the day, you can mark a big X on your calendar. You can also use stickers to track your habit. This will encourage you to do your habit every day, without missing a day because you do not want to break the chain and you do not want to see one day in your calendar without the big X.

Having a visual reminder is a great way to form a good habit. And as the chain grows longer, it will be more difficult to break it because you know that you have already invested a lot of effort in it and breaking it is a big waste of time and effort on your part.

4.Change your environment

Your environment has a big part in developing habits. Consider the Spartans and the Special Operations Units. Their environments are not necessarily comfortable, but they are effective in forming good habits and breaking bad ones. For instance, the beds they sleep in are not exactly hotel material. But it works because it helps them to wake up early every morning and to always be alert, something that they have to do even when they are sleeping.

You also need to learn about the activation energy, or the level of energy required to get something done. The more activation energy is required, the less likely you will do the action and stick to it. And vice versa. For example, if you want to read more books, make sure books are available in every room of your house. If you put away your books in a glass-enclosed shelf with lock and key, then forming the habit of reading will be more difficult. Make it easier for you to do your habit.

5.Be accountable

If you are held accountable for your actions, you are most likely to stick to doing your habits. One good idea is to make your goal public. Tell your family or friends about what you are trying to achieve, whether it is eating healthier, getting more exercise, minimizing impulse buying, waking up early, and so on.

By letting people know about your plans, you will feel more obligated to follow through because you do not want to embarrass yourself and let people think that you are all talk and no substance. You can also find an accountability partner who will help you track your progress and make you stick to your plan.

Remember how the Spartan women treat men while training? They teased and ridiculed men to make them perform well. You do not necessarily need someone to shame you just to make you do what you need to do because that is an extreme method but at least try to find a buddy who will not let you go off track whenever you feel like slacking off.

Soldiers also have buddies while training who help them get through the different tasks but also boosts their morale when they feel down. And you should of course do the same thing to your accountability partner if he is also in the process of developing a new habit.

6.Make it a part of yourself

Habits are a part of a person's identity. You associate the habit to the person and sometimes it is what the person is known for. When someone asks you about your friends, you will say something like, "I have a friend who loves to exercise and goes to the gym every day" or "There's this friend of mine who can't function at all without drinking her cup of coffee first". Or when you are asked to tell more details about yourself, you will probably say something like "I make it a point to finish my important tasks first before I move on to the easier ones". These are all habits and you identify people, including yourself, with them.

If you start thinking of an action as a part of yourself, it will be easier for you to stick to it without the need for constant reinforcement. Make it a part of yourself that makes you a unique individual.

Breaking bad habits

Habits are a part of your normal life, which is why they are difficult to break. Bad habits have always been a subject of psychological studies and research because they have negative impacts on a person's life. It keeps them from achieving their goals and it also interrupts with their life. Bad habits are also not good for your health and they are just a waste of resources including time, energy, and money.

Two of the major causes of bad habits are boredom and stress. Sometimes, people have nothing better to do that they start doing something that later on turns into a bad habit. For example, you go shopping one day because you feel bored and you realized it felt good to buy stuff and it becomes a habit whenever you feel bored. Or sometimes, you feel stressed that you need to do something about it, such as biting your nails. You need to understand the cause of your bad habit and get to the root of the problem so that you can better address it.

So how do you break a bad habit? Here are some ideas.

1.Replace it with a good habit

Sounds easy, but it is actually more difficult than you think. Sometimes, two opposing habits, one good and the other bad, have the same end-result. For instance, you smoke every time you feel stressed out. It calms your nerves. But of course, smoking is not good for your health. So try to find an alternative. Maybe try breathing techniques for relieving stress. Or try meditation.

Another bad habit is opening Facebook when you are feeling bored. Instead of reading useless information in your newsfeed, why not do something else that will challenge you mentally, like reading a book or answering a crossword puzzle. You can even do some short exercises. There are so many alternatives that you can think of. Just identify what triggers your craving that results in bad behavior, and from there, come up with other behaviors that will satisfy that craving.

2. Try to remove triggers

Ask yourself what triggers your habits? Once you determine the trigger, try to cut it to make the bad habit go away. For example, if you find yourself reaching for that bottle of alcohol whenever you feel lonely, it means your trigger is the feeling of loneliness. You can remove that feeling of loneliness by reaching out to your loved ones or learning a hobby, which can replace your habit of drinking. Keep in mind that habit is different from addiction. If you are addicted, which means you are already an alcoholic, you need to seek professional help.

If the sight of clothes at the mall triggers your impulse to buy, then do not go to the mall. You cannot really remove the mall from its location but you can definitely avoid it.

3. Cold turkey solutions might not always work

Doing something cold turkey is doing it right away, without easing yourself gradually into the behavior. For example, if you have been smoking for ten years today, deciding to stop smoking starting tomorrow is a cold turkey solution. You will only find yourself taking a puff after a few days and starting the bad habit again because cold turkey solutions make things into definite black and white areas. This means that it only views the bad habit as something 100% negative, when in fact, bad habits also give something positive. Smoking, for instance, makes a person feel calm and helps relieves stress, although it is definitely bad for the health. This is why it is important to take this into consideration instead of instantly taking away that one thing that makes you feel better.

Moreover, going cold turkey also puts emphasis on perfection. And perfection is something that is difficult to achieve. One mistake that you make already makes your whole plan a failure. Try to give yourself a little wiggle-room especially if you have been doing the habit for many years.

Going cold turkey is not always a failure when it comes to breaking a bad habit. In fact, a lot of people have done it before. Some stopped smoking instantly without giving too much thought about it but they are able to stick to it. These are strong-willed individuals, like the Spartans and the Special Forces. Of course, you can also be like them, if you improve your willpower, which has been discussed in depth in the previous chapters.

You can combine the techniques mentioned in forming good habits with the tips for breaking bad habits. They go hand in hand. And if you do them together, you will find it easier to reach your goals.

You might also want to know the different habits of the Spartans and the Special Forces that make them excellent warriors and soldiers.

Habits of Spartan warriors and elite

soldiers that you should try

Cold shower in the morning

You already know by now that the Spartans took cold showers in the morning. Doing this helped build their iron discipline because it helps your body get used to discomfort. And when your body can endure discomfort, you will not easily give in to temptations and impulses, thus greatly improving your self-discipline. You should also include this in your daily habit if you want to do it the Spartan way.

Always have an escape plan or plan B

Special Forces always survey the place quickly for escape routes in case of an attack or ambush. Although it is not a common occurrence to be attacked, it is still a great habit to develop especially today when the world is a lot more dangerous. Going to your favorite Starbucks might be something that you do on a daily basis and you feel comfortable going to the place but you should learn about emergency exits the next time you go back to buy coffee.

In relation to having an escape plan, you should also have a backup plan or plan B or however you want to call it in case your initial plan didn't work out. For example, if you are thinking about going on a trip abroad, but you are still not sure if you can take off from work for several days, you should have an alternative plan, like going on a local vacation. Preparing for something that could happen apart from your initial plan is something that you should develop into a habit to prevent disappointments and frustrations.

Intermittent fasting

For the Spartan warriors, eating is not done for pleasure. It is a necessity used to fuel their body to finish their training and for when they go to battle. The Spartans didn't wake up in the middle of the night and go to the kitchen for a midnight snack or munch on something when they feel bored. And neither do the Special Forces. They eat because they need to not because they want to. Intermittent fasting is a habit that the Spartans practiced.

While on fasting, your senses will be more sensitive to stimuli and you will be on high alert. After eating, you will feel like resting and you are not in the mood to do anything. This does not mean that you should not eat because of course you need food to live but only eat what your body needs for nourishment. Moreover, a lot of studies show that intermittent fasting is effective if you are trying to lose weight. It surely has a lot of benefits. No wonder the Spartans did it thousands of years ago.

You can try something like not eating anything from 8PM to 12 noon. This is easy because you sleep most of the time during these hours. You can also try doing it alternately, one day you will go fasting and the next you will eat normally. It is up to you what you think will work best but this is a great habit to pick up because it promotes eating only what your body needs and it prevents you from eating unnecessarily.

Start your day early

Soldiers are known for being early risers. You will already see them up and about even before the sun rises. And they are not like most people who are still half asleep after getting up. They are alert and already being productive. Most of them spend the first waking hour of their day running because they want to keep their blood flowing first thing in the morning. Jogging in the morning is not only a good cardio exercise. It also increases your mental alertness throughout the day. It helps you get ready for the day's tasks. Moreover, by waking up early, you will be able to accomplish more and also finish tasks early on.

However, not all people are early risers no matter what they do. They simply function better during nighttime. There's nothing wrong with this, as long as you finish what needs to be done on time. It is just preferred by the military to wake up early because nothing beats getting up early in the morning and jogging outside to the sound of birds chirping and just when the sun is about to rise.

Heavy lifting three times a week

If you want to look like a Spartan warrior or a military man, you should start working on those muscles by lifting heavy weights at least thrice a week. Do not go straight for those small dumbbells, followed by bicep curls. You should follow an effective program for lifting weight, such as Strong-lifts 5x5 that focuses on your strength and size. You should spend your time doing the dead-lift, the bench press, the overhead press, and the squat. Increase the intensity of your workout by adding more weight and counts to your current workout. This will not only improve your physique, strength, and stamina. It will also make you mentally tough because you are able to endure a physical workout of this intensity several days in a week.

Good grooming

This is not about vanity but more about being presentable and respectable-looking. If you want people to take you seriously, you should look the part, especially if you are trying to scare off enemies. You do not necessarily need to buzz cut but always make sure that your hair is trimmed. For guys, long hair only gets in the way and is also difficult to maintain so keep it short at all times. You do not want to waste your time styling your hair every day.

Aside from hair, you should also pay attention to what you wear. Have you seen a soldier wearing wrinkled clothes? Make sure your clothes are ironed before you wear them. Trim your nails regularly because long nails are a no-no. Always strive to look your best wherever you go even when you are at home because when you look good, you will also feel good about yourself which is a great boost of confidence.

8

Fearlessness and Overcoming Fear

One of the many adjectives that describe the Spartans and the elite forces is fearless. They are the very essence of brave and courageous men who are willing to die for their country. Of course, you are just an ordinary person and dying for your country is not really a part of your responsibilities right now but you can definitely learn a thing or two about being fearless from the Greek warriors and elite special operations forces. These people have a lot to fear because their lives are always on the line but they are not afraid of facing the enemies to complete their mission.

This is not exactly about not being scared of ghosts or monsters. You are not a child anymore, after all. This is about conquering your fear of taking on challenges and responsibilities in life because you are afraid that you do not have the capability to succeed. This is also about conquering not only fears but other negativities that you may have in life that prevent you from succeeding.

You probably sometimes think that the quote about fearing nothing other than fear itself is a little too much because there is a lot to fear in life when in fact, this is something that the Spartans and elite forces have to live up to.

The Marine Raiders, Green Berets, Navy Seals, SAS, SBS, and other Special Forces always face dangers. It is not just a quote for them but something that they have to face on a regular basis. It is their job and their life. Of course, ordinary people like you and me do not face the same kind of life-threatening situations like these elite soldiers. But we can learn a thing or two from them when it comes to being fearless.

Overcoming fear has a lot to do with self-discipline. Self-discipline is all about mind over matter, not giving in to impulses and urges that can prove detrimental to your life goals. Being fearless is the same way. It is also about practicing mind over matter because you have to overcome something, and in this case, your fear of whatever it is that scares you.

Here are some lessons that you can learn from elite soldiers who eat dangerous missions for breakfast:

Prepare and practice

The Special Forces and the ancient Spartans train really hard before they become full-fledged soldiers or warriors. The Spartans, for instance, started their preparation at a really young age. Most of their lives were spend training to become the very best Spartan warriors. And it paid off because their reputation as strong and powerful soldiers is still very much known up to this day.

The Special Forces of today also undergo training that would make any Spartan proud. Training is equal to preparation and practice, and according to James Water, a former commander of a Seal platoon, the Navy Seals spend 25% of their time on deployment and 75% goes to training, which includes preparation and practice. If you have prepared enough for what you are about to do, you will lose yourself in the moment and you will not have time to worry and be scared.

One of the objectives of preparation and practice is to know and master what you are about to do. In the case of the elite soldiers, they undergo training to prepare their bodies, mind, and emotions for when they are deployed to accomplish: And that is special tasks or missions. They learn about their goal, the place where they are going to be deployed, their enemy, their plan of attack, their weapons, and other important details of their mission that can help them succeed. They learn everything they can learn about their mission so that when they are deployed, they will not feel scared because they already know what they are about to face.

If you have a presentation and you are scared of public speaking, you have to make sure that you prepare beforehand by researching, writing down notes, practicing in front of the mirror, and knowing and understanding your topic by heart so that you will feel less scared while presenting. You will feel more confident explaining your topic and answering questions that your audience will raise.

Overcoming fear is about being confident. And to be confident, you have to master the task that you need to accomplish to reach your goal by preparing and practicing.

Learn from The Joker

The Joker laughs at his enemies or even when in a situation where ordinary people will feel scared. This is his way of handling his fears. You do not necessarily need to be The Joker who is a little crazy but you can learn from him when it comes to fear management. Laugh at something that scares you or something that you feel you cannot do. This makes your fear or doubts seem insignificant and silly. It also tells you that everything will be fine and things will work out in the end.

This is also a technique that the Navy Seals and Army Rangers do when they find themselves in a dangerous situation. And there is scientific basis for this. A research conducted by the Stanford University showed that people who made jokes after looking at disturbing pictures coped a lot better than people who did not about what they saw.

If you feel scared about cutting back on all the things that you are used to having but don't really need, such as your daily dose of Starbucks coffee or your monthly shopping spree, you should just look at it as something funny and frivolous, which will make it easier for you to do them. If you feel afraid of going into the shower without hot water, you should make a joke about it or laugh at yourself for being scared of something so silly and you will feel your fear go away.

The world may be a scary place, but if you find humor in any situation, even the scary and difficult ones, you will go very far.

Let it go

Okay, this is not about that Disney movie but this can help a lot when it comes to overcoming your fear. Colonel David M. Benedek, M.D. believes that talking about one's fears is a great way to overcome fear itself because it helps you understand your fear more.

Soldiers who are in a dangerous situation are encouraged to talk to their peers while on deployment to help them find meaning in what they do. After deployment, when the soldiers return to their homes, they are encouraged to talk to experts or undergo therapy because it helps them make sense of what they have experienced while on deployment. These soldiers have seen and experienced a lot of traumatic things that will make any ordinary person be scarred for life but talking about it at least diminishes the feeling of fear.

You can talk to someone you trust, like a close friend or family, if you have fears that you would like to overcome. For example, if you are planning to quit smoking cigarettes but you are scared of taking the leap because smoking has been a big part of your life since you were a teenager, then you can talk about it to someone close to you.

Amitting your fear to someone, and hearing yourself voicing it out loud, is a great way to confront your fear because you are letting it out in the open. Do not keep it bottled up inside like shitty booze. Tell someone about it and let it all go and you will realize that sometimes, fear is just all in your head.

Take deep breaths

Some people show physical manifestations of fear. You will feel their heart beating faster and you will see them sweating bullets. Some also feel their knees turning to jelly and their voice shaking when they start to speak. When you start to feel and see these physical signs of fear on yourself, just breathe slowly and deeply.

You already know by now that elite soldiers use breathing techniques to calm their nerves. It also allows them to control the physical manifestations of fear. And when they feel that they are in control, they will feel more powerful and fearless. A Navy Seal trainer even said that breathing is like a software that helps you bend your hardware or your body. It may sound too nerdy but this is in fact what breathing does to your body. It allows you to get a grip on yourself and continue doing what you need to do without showing signs that you are scared or nervous.

Ignore the voice in your head

As discussed previously, fear is all in your head. It is just about mind over matter. If other people can do it, so can you. When you start to hear that negative voice in your head telling you that you cannot do it, make it stop by simply ignoring. You are probably wondering why do we have this kind of inner voice that gives us feelings of fear and nervousness in times of stress. Why can't we have an inner voice that acts like a cheerleader instead, a voice that tells us that we can do it. Apparently, this is how our brains work. It simply gives us the worst-case scenarios when that's the last thing you need.

Do you know what elite soldiers do when the negative self-talk starts inside their heads? They ignore the voice. Or if you have an asshole inner voice that is really persistent, you might want to do something more drastic, such as mentally shouting over the negative thoughts and replacing them with positive thoughts. To do this, you need to focus on the positive aspects of the task or situation. If you are feeling nervous or scared about talking in front of a large group of people, you can simply remind yourself that this will improve your grades or give you a shot at being promoted. It takes self-discipline to do this because you have to exert willpower so that the negative self-talk will not prevail.

Courage versus boldness

You need to know the difference between the two because they are sometimes used interchangeably when, in fact, they are not exactly the same. Let's understand more about these terms by looking at the two powerful ancient Greek cities—Athens and Sparta. We all know that between the two, the Spartans were better at warfare because of many reasons. They had extreme discipline and their training was so effective that modern warfare training and techniques are patterned after the Spartan's Agoge system.

So what is it about the Spartans that the Athenians lacked? What made them far superior, that later on led to the defeat and decline of Athens? The answer is in the character trait that these ancient people embodied. The Spartans had andreia, or courage, while the Athenians had thrasytes, or boldness.

Courage means bravery and it involves manliness. It is one characteristic of a mature man. Courage and manliness are intertwined. One can achieve courage when one has achieved maturity. On the other hand, boldness is seen more as a boyish trait. A bold man is highly ambitious, brazen, and proud. Whereas a brave or courageous man is calm, steady, and God-fearing. Between the two, who do you think is more reliable, the brave man or the bold man? Obviously, you would want someone courageous to be on your side during combat, or in dire situations, because you can definitely rely on them. Or better yet, be the courageous man that every man should strive to be.

Boldness is impulsive and sometimes even reckless. It does not involve thinking and analyzing of situations and facts. Of course, this trait can be beneficial, too, when in the context of seizing a great opportunity that knocks on your door only once in a lifetime. In this case, boldness can be used, but it should still be coupled with courage and self-discipline all throughout. And a man should always strive to be courageous than bold.

Courage is enduring and steady, it can endure suffering for a longer period of time. It is also humble and has its feet always planted firmly on the ground. This is why courage is more pleasing to heaven.

Boldness, on the other hand, is impatient and fickle. It cannot endure sufferings especially for long periods of time, and the prize or victory should be instant; otherwise, boldness will die. This is why courage involves self-discipline because it does not give in to impulse but rather it delays gratification for a much better reward. Because boldness is impatient, its main weakness is time, it cannot endure, and is easily perishable.

The Athenians were known for their surprise attacks and quick battles that had a decisive result. The Spartans, on the other hand, were known for their endurance and strength in prolonged battles. For the Athenians, when victory did not come easily, they lose heart and hope, and they give up. This quality and mindset, which works excellently with self-discipline, are what made the

Spartans more superior than the Athenians.

Today, you see a lot of people who are more bold than courageous. Sure, they get excited about the idea of tackling a new task or starting a new habit, but this excitement and the burning passion of doing something new only lasts for a short time. The first few days are fun and exciting; they write down their tasks and even track their activities. But as time goes by, when the novelty of the idea wears off and when setbacks arrive, the feeling of excitement slowly fades—it will plateau then slowly go into a downward spiral. It becomes boring, and they realize that it involves a lot of hard work that they did not anticipate.

As days go by, they start working less and less on the task. Before, they did it every day. After a couple of months, they just did it a few times a week, then whenever they feel like doing it, then at last, they just start to completely ignore it. These people will come up with excuses—they are working on other stuff, they are too busy, they do not feel good anymore working on that task. A lot of excuses. They will even go as far as telling themselves that this task is the wrong task for them in the first place because doing it feels so difficult. And shouldn't it be more fun, especially since they've been doing it for quite some time now? They make themselves believe that the task is wrong for them. When in fact, it is their work ethic that is the problem. They do not have the self-discipline and courage to continue what they have started.

If you have the mindset of the Athenians, who did not finish what they started, and who just leave things when the going gets tough, you should change your ways because this will only lead to your downfall, like what happened to the Athenians. It will become a cycle that is more difficult to get out of. Be more like the Spartans, who will start a task and make sure that they see it through till the end. Boldness can help you start things, but only courage can make you finish.

9

Lessons Learned from the Spartans and Special Forces

There are a lot of things you can learn from the Spartans and the Special Forces, the people who epitomize self-discipline. Based on the topics discussed in this book, here are the lessons that you can learn from these strong and powerful people that you can apply to your own life.

When you do something, do it extremely well

If you have a task or a chore that needs to be done, give it your best shot or don't try at all. The Spartans and Special Forces should be excellent at what they do because it is a matter of life and death. Moreover, it's not just their neck or their team's lives that hang on the balance but also the future of their country. This is why for these people, there are no room for mistakes most of the time. You are just wasting your time if you do something halfheartedly because you might just need to do everything all over again, which is a waste or time, energy, and sometimes money.

You should also avoid being a jack of all trades and master of none. Instead, focus on one thing first before you tackle other tasks so that your attention is not divided into different things which can lead to mistakes.

In other Greek cities including Athens, people could be whatever they wanted to be—farmers, blacksmiths, bakers, fishermen, butchers, and so on. However, when time came when the city had to face its enemies, these people had to leave their normal jobs and became soldiers for their cities. And you very well know that this didn't work. With the Spartans, and elite forces, they were trained solely for the purpose of defending their country or completing missions for their country. The Spartans left these other jobs for people who were not training in the military and they recruited their best and strongest men to become warriors. They did not have a regular job apart from being a warrior or soldier, which made them become masters at what they do.

According to history, the Spartan's power was so great and they were feared by their peers. It was even said that one Spartan soldier is equivalent to several men who came from other cities of Greece.

Keep it simple

The Spartans and the Special Forces always find themselves in dire situations, and they try to employ the simplest actions to get themselves out of this predicament. The simpler the solution is, the better. The Spartans were known for their contempt for long-winded speeches. They would prefer it if you go directly to the point.

At that time, long rhetoric and speeches were extremely popular in Greece especially in Athens but the Spartans did not like this at all because they thought it was a waste of time. They'd rather be doing something more productive than listening to someone's useless ramblings and babbles. So apart from their intense training, the Spartans were also known for their straightforward and simple speeches, sometimes made more interesting by their acerbic wit. This is called laconic speech (Sparta is located in the area called Laconia).

Being simple at everything that you do requires strong self-discipline because people sometimes have this tendency to add fluff or other unnecessary things that do not really do anything to the overall value of something. As they say, less is more and this is true for the Spartans and Special Forces.

Avoid Excessiveness

The Spartans and elite soldiers are also known for their austerity, as explained in the previous point. Let's look at how the Special Forces are trained. When they train, do you think they have extra pillows for comfort? Or do you think their food include yummy treats like cakes or filet mignon? The answer is no. They make do with the basic minimum required to survive.

Their food is nutritious because their body has to be in top shape while training and while on deployment but it does not have extra treats. And this is good because having an excess of anything is detrimental to their situation when they are in combat. Who would want to bring extra things that are not really needed to survive when on deployment? No one because it is just added weight and excess of anything only creates a distraction.

The Spartans also admired craftsmanship but only if it has a practical use.

One example is the Spartan's roof beams. Their law required them to keep the shape of the log as is, without adding finishing touches. Athenians, on the other hand, loved beautiful and luxurious things, and their roof beams are shaped like squares with fine details. When a Spartan visited the house of an Athenian, he was curious about the roof beam. He asked, "Do trees in Athens grow in square shapes? "The Athenian replied, no of course not." Then why would you make them square? Would you make them round if they grew square?" To the Spartan, it was unnecessary to make the roof beam square and it seemed a little excessive because it was a waste of time, energy, and money.

There is another story that shows the austerity of the Spartans in another context. In 479 BCE, the Spartans, together with their Greek allies defeated the Persians at Plataea, a city in Greece. They acquired a lot of things from the Persians including King Xerxes' opulent pavilions. The pavilions were outfitted with hundreds of servants including cooks and wine stewards. The Spartan Regent Pausanius ordered the Persian cooks to whip up dinner for them, something that King Xerxes normally eats. He also ordered his own cooks to prepare a standard Spartan dinner. When the cooks were done, Pausanius and his peers were surprised at the difference between the two dinners.

The Persians prepared a lavish banquet that had several courses including scrumptious sweets and treats for dessert. The food was also served on plates made of gold and the finest wines were offered. On the other hand, the Spartan chefs cooked barley bread and a soup made of pig's blood and vinegar. Pausaius couldn't help but laugh when he saw the two standard dinner fares. He commented that the Persians had to travel far just to rob the Spartans of their poverty.

Living like the Spartans and the elite soldiers requires strong self-discipline because you will sometimes feel like you are lacking something when in fact, you have everything you need. If you see these unnecessary things in life as just that, unnecessary excesses, it will be easier for you to let go of them and just focus on what you truly need in life.

Wanting vs. willing

What is the difference between these two words? Wanting denotes something that you wish to achieve, which means it is more focused on the outcome or results. Willing, on the other hand, denotes taking action. It is more focused on the processes involved to reach your objective. When you write a book, you want to be published. But are you willing to put in a lot of hours and energy researching, reading, and writing?

When you start a new business, you want it to be profitable. But are you willing to invest your time, energy, and money to keep it going? When you start your diet plan, you want to lose weight. But are you willing to give up eating junk foods and go to the gym regularly? It is easy to know what we want in life, but are you willing to compromise, sacrifice, and face difficulties and challenges along the way to reach your goals?

This is also about taking risks. You want to earn money by starting a business but you cannot be a great entrepreneur if you are not willing to take risks. And risks are uncertainties in life, something that you cannot avoid because uncertainties are always there. What you can do is to always do the right action no matter what you risk or uncertainty you are facing. This is why they say that honor comes from uncertainty and not from a favorable outcome because uncertainty tests your character and self-respect.

King Leonidas and his great Spartan warriors knew that if you want to achieve great outcomes, you have to take risks. And aside from honor, this was also where real courage was tested for the Spartans. They did not know what the outcome would be but they were willing to die for their city. And because of this, they came out of the battle victorious.

Teamwork

The Spartans and the Special Forces are two perfect examples of how teamwork should look like. Elite soldiers, for instance, find themselves in dangerous situations and they have no one else to rely on except the other soldiers in their team. Moreover, the success of their operation relies not just on one person but on the whole team. They trained and lived with a group of people before being deployed to wherever they are needed.

The Spartans also lived with other soldiers in communal messes at the young age of 7. And when they finished the Agoge system at the age of 20, they then became citizens of the state and a member of a club which was made up of 15 members who are already citizens in one team. They formed a camaraderie and a special bond and they learned to rely on each other. They called each other 'equals' because they do the same things and they were also taught that when in infantry line, all the soldiers were equal, none was more superior than the others. And each member of the team is responsible for his comrade.

Embrace hardship

The main objective of a civilized life is to be comfortable at all times. A lot of things are invented for this reason. For example, stores that are open 24/7 are so popular because people can buy whatever they want or need anytime of the day. Online shopping is also a convenient way to shop because you do not need to go to the physical store with crowds of people just to buy things. Making your bed can be a hassle because of the many things that you need to put such as pillows, pillow cases, duvet, flat sheet, blanket, and so on. These things are considered necessities in modern society because it makes sleeping a lot more comfortable.

There's nothing wrong with being comfortable. It only becomes a problem when you get so used to it that you forget how to deal with difficulties and challenges in life. Have you every wondered why there are more people in developed countries who suffer from depression than in developing countries? One reason could be that these people who live in rich nations live comfortably and have nothing to think about and work hard for anymore. People in poor countries experience hardships in life and they have no time to wallow in self-pity because they need their wits to survive.

The Spartans and the elite soldiers embrace hardships because this is what makes them strong. This is what makes them so great at what they do. If you want to be like them, you should also look at hardships in a positive light and embrace it because it will make you a better person in the end.

Never give up

Giving up or surrender is not in the vocabulary of the Special Forces Units, and also the Spartans. If the Navy Seals gave up, they would have never caught Bin Laden. If the Spartans gave up, they would never have defeated the Persians. It is simply out of the question. When the Spartan warriors left their home to fight in combat, their mothers or wives would tell them "With it or on it!" This means that the soldiers should either go back home with their shield with them, meaning they were victorious or go back home with their bodies on the shield having died with honor while in combat. Fleeing and running back home leaving their shield behind is not an option because their reputation will forever be tarnished.

Going back to the battle of Thermopylae in 480 BCE, King Leonidas was with his troop composed of 300 Spartans and 7,000 soldiers from other Greek states, guarding the narrow mountain pass at Thermopylae against the Persian invaders which were composed of around 100,000 to150,000 soldiers. The Persians greatly outnumbered the Greeks, and King Xerxes told the Greeks that they would spare them their lives if they give up their arms. King Leonidas agreed, but on the third day, he realized that the Persians betrayed them, so he ordered the rest of his troops to leave. The Spartans stayed behind and fought the Persians until the end, despite having no weapons and being greatly outnumbered.

Your situations are less extreme than what the Spartans faced during their time but you can learn something valuable from these great people, that even when the odds are against you, you still keep going, you give it all you've got, and you never give up.

10

Daily Self-Discipline—Applying What You Have Learned in Your Everyday Life

Now that you know everything there is to know about the self-discipline of the Spartans and elite forces, the next step is to apply what you have learned in your daily life. No matter who you are or what kind of work you do, the principles and systems presented in this book can still be applied for you to reach your goal in life. Here are some examples on how you can tackle different goals using the approach, habit, and system of the Spartans and the Special Operations Units.

Diet and exercise

You know by now that the Spartans and Special Forces are probably some of the strongest and most powerful men in the world. Their bodies do not have excess fat which is why they can move fast and are very agile. The most effective way to lose weight is to watch and change what you eat. The Spartans and the elite forces eat only because it is necessary to feed their body.

The Spartans, for instance, did not like excessive food and they only ate the bare minimum that their body needed. Like what was mentioned earlier about the story of the Persian and the Spartan chefs, anything lavish is considered excessive.

If you want to eat like the Spartans, include mainly Mediterranean and Greek food in your diet such as olives, figs, avocados, grapes, fish, turkey, chicken, wild rice, and whole-grain bread. You should also cook in olive oil. Of course, you do not necessarily need to copy what the Spartan warriors ate (barley bread and soup made of vinegar and pig's blood) but you get the idea.

Eat food rich in protein to build your muscles. You should consume 1.2 grams of protein for every pound of your total weight. Carbohydrates are also needed in the morning because it acts as the fuel for the day ahead, especially if you are going to do heavy physical tasks. Eat healthy carbohydrates only such as rice and sweet potatoes.

Calorie counting is not really mandatory but the main idea is to eat only the minimum that will give you energy and make sure that your calories come from nutritious food and not from junk food like chips, cakes, and so on. Let go of these junk foods because they contribute nothing to your weight loss goal and they are seen as excessive by the Spartan standards.

Aside from eating only the bare minimum, you should also incorporate workout to your weight loss goal because diet and exercise go hand in hand. A standard workout should include:

- 50 push-ups
- 25 pull-ups
- 50 24-inch box jumps
- 50 deadlifts using a 135-lb barbell
- 50 floor wiper abs exercises
- 50 single-arm clean-and-press using a 36-lb kettlebell

These may seem too much especially if it is your first time to go to the gym but this can definitely help you lose weight. Besides, the Spartans and the Special Forces had more difficult workouts than this so just suck it up and do what you got to do. You can also do it gradually. Start with fewer repetitions at first then add more as you get used to the exercises.

And the most important thing to remember is that it starts in your mind. Did you know that professional athletes visualize the end result of their workout to give them motivation not only to start but also to finish? The brain is so powerful that if you are given a placebo and you are told that it can cure your disease, your disease will be cured because you believed in it even though the placebo does not really have any medical properties, aside from tricking your brain into believing something.

Morning routine

Having a morning routine is the best way to start your day because it conditions your brain every day. It also makes you more efficient and productive throughout the day. Your morning routine does not simply start in the morning. You have to consider your nighttime routine as well, which includes planning the next day's activities and sleeping early.

Sleeping early makes it easier for you to get out of bed early in the morning. Stop using your phone and browsing online before you go to bed because it makes your mind awake, which makes it difficult for you to fall asleep. This is why many people end up wasting several hours of their time just watching senseless videos and looking at funny memes. Once you start, it is difficult to stop so it is best not to start browsing at all especially when you are in bed.

The main benefit of having a morning routine is that you are preparing yourself, your mind and your body for the day ahead. It allows you to start your day right, with your best foot forward. If you start your day right, the rest of the day will be more productive. The morning routine is priming your mind to take on all the challenges that you will be facing throughout the day. It is like your mind's fuel that will help you finish all the tasks you need to do.

Former Navy Seal soldiers still wake up as early as 4:30 AM even when they are no longer in service because they know the benefit of waking up before everyone else. The culture of responsibility and self-discipline is called extreme ownership, a phrase coined by former Navy SEAL commander Jocko Willink. He now works with large companies such as Citibank and Shell Oil to train people about leadership and self-discipline. Together with another former commander Leif Babin, they formed a consulting firm called Echelon Front.

Of course, they believe in the phrase practice what you preach. So for them to teach discipline, they have to practice discipline themselves. Sure, their past experiences as platoon commanders count but it is still better to teach something that are still major parts of their lives.

Waking up early has practical benefits, such as having some free time all to yourself that makes it easier for you to take care of things that you feel are important. For example, if getting in shape is important to you and you cannot find the time during the day to work out, you can do it early in the morning. No one can take that time away from you because everyone else is still asleep—your family, your boss, your friends.

If you work out at, say, 6 PM after work, your wife may suddenly call you and ask you to come home early because of an emergency or your boss might call you regarding your report. These things can chip away at your time to work out, and before you know it, you will end up not working out at all. If you do it at 4:30 AM, no one will bother you because they are most likely still sleeping.

Aside from the practical benefit, waking up early also helps you develop self-discipline. When you hear your alarm at 4:30 AM, it is so tempting to stay snuggled under your blankets and go back to sleep. It is so difficult to wake up early. But fighting these urges is a step towards achieving stronger self-discipline. And when you wake up early, you will definitely have a better day because your mind is free from worrying about things that you could have done in the morning and your mind is clear and sharp.

Let's say you decide to wake up at 5 AM. For five minutes, make your entire body alert from head to toe by doing some stretches. Afterward, drink 2 glasses of water, make and drink coffee, and prepare to go to the gym. All of these should be done by 5:30. From 5:30 to 7 AM, drive to the gym and start your workout. The workout is at least one hour. You can also do some meditation for about 45 minutes after you work out your body.

Do this routine every day and you will see improvements not only in your body but also in your mindset.

Finances and budget

Self-discipline is an important trait when it comes to managing your finances. If you do not have self-discipline, you will end up with a lot of debt that you cannot pay. Be more like the Spartans and also the Special Forces by practicing restraint, especially when you go shopping.

In today's world that encourages capitalism, you sometimes feel left out when you do not have the latest of everything. It may be more difficult to be more frugal when all the people around you always buy things, but you have to stick to your objective if you want to save up for the future and be financially independent.

Keep in mind that being frugal is a virtue and it is completely different from being a cheapskate. Sometimes, people think that those who are careful with their money are cheap, tightwads, or stingy when this is not the case. Being frugal, like the Spartans, mean spending money wisely or on things that matter in life.

For example, a frugal person will buy nutritious food that the body needs but a cheapskate will buy whatever is the cheapest even if it does not have any nutritional value. A frugal person also does not like wastage, not just in terms of money but also when it comes to other aspects of life. A cheapskate, on the other hand, does not care about wastage as long as he is not spending his own money on it. Being frugal means buying things that add value to your overall life and well-being.

The way of the Spartans when it comes to managing finances requires acting generously, ethically, and honorably. For example, bringing home office supplies that your kids can use for school is not honorable and this is how cheapskates behave. A frugal person will not stoop to this kind of behavior. When a frugal person invites a friend whom he hasn't seen for a long time to meet for dinner, he will graciously offer to pay because he's the one who made the invitation, whereas a cheapskate will probably ask his friend to pay for what he ate. A frugal person is also never selfish. Sure, he will spend money on himself from time to time but he would rather spend his money on his loved ones.

Financial independence also gives you the ability to control your time. For example, if you know you have enough savings in your bank for retirement, you can retire early and spend your days doing things that you love like learning a new hobby or traveling. On the other hand, if you have a lot of debts to pay, you know that you cannot afford to stop working because you have to pay for our debt, which means that you are spending most of your time working instead of doing things that you really love to do.

The mindset of a frugal person is spending intelligently and being mindful of his purchases. And making intelligent choices is something that he applies not only on his spending habits but also on every aspect of his life.

What you can do is to write down all aspects of your finances—your earnings every month and your expenses. Your expenses can be further divided into fixed expenses such as mortgage and flexible expenses such as utility bills. You also need to include emergency money and savings. Make sure that your monthly earning is bigger than your monthly expenses. If you are spending more than you are earning, you will incur debts. If this is the case, you have to figure out what you can do to pay off your debts. One solution is to cut back on unnecessary expenses. This includes your shopping sprees every time the season changes to buy new clothes or your cable subscription. You can simply reuse your clothes and you can just watch movies and series on Netflix, which costs a lot less.

Aside from cutting back on your expenditures, you should also think about earning more money. Maybe you can sell your old clothes since you are trying to be more like the Spartans and Special Forces who most likely do not have a lot of clothes. Or you can offer services, such as teaching English online or babysitting.

Again, being frugal and changing how you spend requires self-discipline. It may be difficult at first, but just hang in there because you will soon realize the benefits of being frugal when you start to experience financial independence.

Material possessions

If you are a man trying to pursue his life goals every day, you want your space to be in order at all times. This is why the Spartans and Special Operations Units are the ultimate minimalists when it comes to owning material possessions. If your home is free from clutter, you will have fewer distractions that can prevent you from achieving your goals. A man who is in pursuit of his very best every single day will surely have a few nice things that he considers important but compared to others, his possessions are a lot fewer because he believes in the saying that less is more.

It was discussed earlier that the Spartans and the elite forces do not like anything excessive. They thrive on simplicity and austerity. For these strong and self-disciplined men, the desire to accumulate material things is shallow and immature, especially when they are put on display to be admired by others. They believe that if a person relies on material wealth to be happy and to know his personal wealth, he is a weak person. It is a weakness or a flaw in character that you should try to avoid.

During the ancient times, when most Greek cities were interested in opulent buildings and large monuments, the Spartans were sometimes seen as less cultured, even though they were just as civilized and as interested in culture and the arts. This is the very reason why most people are scared to let go of their material possessions. They are afraid that people will see them as poor or uncultured. They don't like the feeling of being left behind. The Spartans simply did not care because it was ingrained in them from the beginning that anything excessive was not good and these were frowned upon in their own city. Their principles and convictions were a major part of their upbringing that these trivial things do not bother them anymore.

Of course, there is nothing wrong with enjoying nice and even luxurious things in life but do not make your life revolve around it and do not use it to measure your value as a person. Material possessions only become bad when in excess and when you put too much value in them.

What you can do is to stop buying things that you do not really need. This is hitting two birds with one stone because you are not adding clutter to your life and at the same time you are saving money. Aside from not accumulating things, you should also consider letting go of things that you no longer need. These can be your old clothes, books, and so on. Throw them out, give them to friends or family, donate them, or sell them. Just leave behind the things that you only need and the things that make you happy. If you haven't used it in months, chances are you will not use it at all. When you declutter your home, you are also decluttering your life.

Choosing wisely is also another way you can do to downgrade. If you are single and have no family, why buy a large SUV when you are just going to use it driving yourself to work? Just buy a small sedan. Or better yet, you can skip buying a car altogether and just use the metro or bus if you live in a city like New York.

These are the ways of the Spartans and the Special Forces. You can be like them if you follow all the tips and techniques explained in this book. The outcome is a better life, a life worth living.

Conclusion

Thank you for reading the book *Self-Discipline: The Spartans and Special*

Operations Way To Mastering Yourself. You already know that self-discipline should be practiced in every action and decision that you make because it is one of the first steps to achieving your goals in life.

Hopefully, this book helps you change your daily routine and improve the overall quality of your life. The result may not be instantaneous but that is what self-discipline is all about—delaying gratification for a much bigger reward. And in this case, your reward is a better you and a better life.

Thank You

Finally, if you enjoyed this book, then I'd like to ask you for a favor. Would you be kind enough to leave a review for this book on Amazon? It'd be greatly appreciated!

Thank you and good luck!

Copyright

of the trademark is without permission or backing by the trademark owner. All trademarks and brands within this book are for clarifying purposes only and are the owned by the owners themselves, not affiliated with this document.

Printed in Great Britain
by Amazon

59077953R00073